Valuation for
Financial Reporting

Valuation for Financial Reporting

Intangible Assets, Goodwill, and
Impairment Analysis, SFAS 141 and 142

Michael J. Mard, CPA/ABV, ASA
James R. Hitchner, CPA/ABV, ASA
Steven D. Hyden, CPA, ASA
Mark L. Zyla, CPA/ABV, ASA, CFA

John Wiley & Sons, Inc.

ISBN 0-471-23753-1

Printed in the United States of America

10 9 8 7 6 5 4 3 2

Contents

To our families—
near and far;
young and old;
those who have come to us recently;
those who have gone before us;
we love you and thank you.
It is with your support
all things, including this book,
are possible.

Preface

We have written this book to provide guidance and insight in the identification, measurement, and management of intangible assets and goodwill pursuant to the Financial Accounting Standards Board (FASB) Statement of Financial Accounting Standards (SFAS) No. 141, *Business Combinations,* and SFAS No. 142, *Goodwill and Other Intangible Assets.*

Case studies are provided presenting the application of purchase accounting under SFAS No. 141 and a goodwill impairment study under SFAS No. 142. Related issues such as the American Institute of Certified Public Accountants (AICPA) Practice Aid Series, *Assets Acquired in a Business Combination to Be Used in Research and Development Activities: A Focus of Software, Electronic Devices, and Pharmaceutical Industries* (IPR&D Practice Aid), are covered.

SFAS Nos. 141 and 142 require financial statements of a surviving company to reflect the true financial impact of a merger or acquisition and mandate the use of the purchase method of accounting by eliminating the pooling of interests method for all business combinations. Application of the purchase method requires identification of all assets of the acquiring enterprise, tangible and intangible. In addition, any excess of the cost of an acquired entity over the net amounts assigned to the tangible and intangible assets acquired, and the liabilities assumed, is classified as goodwill.

This book is designed to bring clarity to what will be a challenge for financial executives, certified public accountants (CPAs), and valuation analysts. Because of the new requirements of reporting intangible assets and goodwill, they will not only have to focus on determining fair value of the assets acquired, but also must assess on at least an annual basis whether impairment of those assets has occurred. This book explains the valuation aspects of the new financial reporting requirements, including how to identify the characteristics of goodwill and intangible assets, determine if impairment has occurred, and employ specific methods to assess the financial impact of such impairment.

Readers are provided an example of a business combination in which tangible and intangible assets are identified and measured, starting with the determination of the purchase price and development of a business enterprise analysis. These preliminary steps establish the magnitude of the total value to be allocated (if you will, the size of the whole pie). The allocation of fair value to the individual assets (determining the size of each slice) will require identifying and quantifying the various types of intangible assets acquired including: technology-based, customer-related, marketing-related, contract-based, and goodwill.

The cost approach to valuation will be demonstrated for software, customer relationships, and assembled workforce. Various methods of the income approach will be used to determine value of a noncompete agreement, trade name, technology, and in-process research and development. Goodwill arises if there is any residual value after deducting the value of all other assets from the purchase price.

A detailed example of an impairment analysis is also provided. The case study covers determination of fair value for reporting units and the effect on the first step of an impairment analysis. Step two determines the extent of goodwill impairment and is calculated by subtracting from the new fair value of the reporting unit the new fair values of the tangible and intangible assets.

Significant issues related to SFAS No. 142 are addressed including: treatment of previously identified but unbooked intangible assets subsumed in goodwill, determination of what constitutes a reporting unit, and treatment and allocation of synergies resulting from the business combination and subsequent impairment.

Also, included in Chapter 7 are a checklist for data gathering and a work program designed to guide the public or private practitioner through the maze of methodologies which may be employed in the determination of the value of intangibles. In-process research and development (IPR&D) receives special attention with the inclusion of the AICPA Best Practices Audit Program delineating procedures to be considered when auditing a business combination transaction that may involve IPR&D.

We have presented a limited discussion on disclosure in the appendix to Chapter 4 only. We have not presented detailed disclosure discussions; we believe such matters to be corporate and audit decisions unique to each company's financial statement presentation. Nor have we presented time lines for implementation; the Statements are effective now. Excluding these two areas allowed a more concise and in-depth review of the regulations' impact. Our goal has been to provide a concise and understandable explanation of the regulatory and conceptual issues underlying SFAS Nos. 141 and 142. Due to the highly technical nature of this area and the importance of the phrasing as originally presented in the standards and their interpretation, we decided to extract much of the text as is. We are grateful to those who recognized the regulatory importance of this and granted permission to quote their materials.

While numerous articles and commentaries on the subject have appeared dating back to the time the FASB began considering the issue, we believe our book is the first to provide real world examples of the valuation techniques and methodologies required to perform a purchase price allocation under SFAS No. 141 and an impairment study under SFAS No. 142. The authors hope that *Valuation for Financial Reporting* will help lift the veil of mystery surrounding these two important pronouncements and provide a practical guide for their implementation.

Acknowledgments

To Faye Danger and Deanna Muraki: Faye, thank you for your diligent editing and your tenacity in rooting out virtually every glitch. Thanks for your perseverance and keeping us on the straight and narrow. Deanna, without your information processing skills, Faye wouldn't have anything to edit. Thanks for taking our rambling, disjointed squiggles and turning them into a finished product.

We also thank Robert R. Dunne, for his strategic perspective and insight, and his lovely wife, Linda, who made his insights readable. We thank our editor, John DeRemigis, for getting Wiley's formidable support and our partners and staff for keeping the wheels turning while we were elsewhere engaged.

We wish to thank our reviewers for their many comments and suggestions for improving this first edition. From the Financial Consulting Group, they are recognized Specialists in Financial Reporting: Neil J. Beaton, CPA/ABV, CFA, ASA; Darren S. Cordier, CFA; Robert E. Duffy, CPA/ABV, CFA, ASA; William I. Nickles, ASA; James S. Rigby, CPA/ABV, ASA; and Thomas A. Yermack, CFA.

From the national accounting firms, those firms that most directly carry the burden of self-regulating the accurate implementation of SFAS Nos. 141 and 142, we thank R. Gregory Morris, CPA of KPMG Consulting, Inc. and James Alerding, CPA/ABV, ASA, CVA, with Clifton Gunderson, LLP

From academia, we thank Joseph E. McCann, III, Ph.D., Dean of Sykes College of Business at the University of Tampa, for his comments and support, and particularly for his energy in spearheading the recognition, measurement, and management of intangible assets specific to hitech companies in Florida.

Special thanks is given to the American Institute of Certified Public Accountants (AICPA) and the Financial Accounting Standards Board (FASB). Portions of various documents, copyrighted by the AICPA, Harborside Financial Center, 201 Plaza Three, Jersey City, NJ 07311-3881, are reprinted with permission. Portions of various documents, copyrighted by the Financial Accounting Standards Board, 401 Merritt 7, P.O. Box 5116, Norwalk, Connecticut 06856-5116, are reprinted with permission. Complete copies of the documents are available from the AICPA and the FASB.

The subject matter is difficult, complex, and interwoven. That is our attempt at setting the stage for excusing any and all mistakes which, despite everyone else's formidable attempts, are universally our burden to carry.

About the Authors

Michael J. Mard, CPA/ABV, ASA is a managing director of The Financial Valuation Group (FVG) in Tampa, Florida. FVG is a financial advisory services firm specializing in valuation and litigation services. He was founding president of The Financial Consulting Group L.C. (FCG), a national association of professional service firms dedicated to excellence in valuation, litigation, and financial consulting.

Mr. Mard is an FCG recognized specialist for "Financial Reporting in Intangible Assets and Goodwill Impairment." He was ad hoc advisor to the FASB on their deliberations concerning SFAS Nos. 141 and 142 and presented them a session on valuing and lifing intangible assets. Mr. Mard has coauthored 20 courses, published over 60 articles, taught 30 courses and been a presenter and speaker on more than 40 occasions.

Mr. Mard has been a full-time business appraiser and expert witness for over 18 years, specializing in intangible assets, specifically intellectual property. He has developed analyses that have been reviewed and accepted by the Securities and Exchange Commission, numerous accounting firms (including the Big Five), the IRS, and the courts.

Mr. Mard is very active at state and national levels with emphasis on business valuation standards and intellectual property valuations. He coauthored the AICPA Consulting Services Practice Aid 99-2, "Valuing Intellectual Property and Calculating Infringement Damages" and has served on numerous committees and task forces of the AICPA, FICPA, FASB, and ASA. He has received the AICPA Business Volunteer of the Year award and has been inducted into the AICPA Business Valuation Hall of Fame.

James R. Hitchner, CPA/ABV, ASA is a shareholder and co-CEO with Phillips Hitchner (PH) in Atlanta, Georgia, which is a financial advisory services firm that specializes in valuation and litigation services and is a founding member of the Financial Consulting Group, L.C. (FCG). FCG is a national association of professional services firms dedicated to excellence in valuation, financial, and litigation consulting.

Mr. Hitchner is an FCG recognized specialist for "Financial Reporting in Intangible Assets and Goodwill Impairment." He has been involved in hundreds of intangible asset valuations and has presented his work to the SEC on numerous occasions. He was ad hoc advisor to the FASB on their deliberations concerning SFAS Nos. 141 and 142 and presented them a session on valuing and lifing intangible assets.

Mr. Hitchner has more than 23 years of professional experience, including 21 years in valuation services and two years in real estate development. Prior to forming PH in 1995, he was partner-in-charge of valuation services for the Southern Region of Coopers & Lybrand (now PriceWaterhouseCoopers), where he spent more than nine years. He has been recognized as a qualified expert witness, and has provided testimony on valuations in Florida, Georgia, Indiana, New Jersey, North Carolina, Ohio, Tennessee, and Virginia.

Mr. Hitchner has coauthored 10 courses, taught over 30 courses, published over 20 articles, and has made over 70 conference presentations. He is also an inductee in the AICPA Business Valuation Hall of Fame. He is past chairman of the Business Valuation Committee of the Georgia Society of CPAs, past member of the AICPA Business Valuation Subcommittee, and current member of the AICPA task force on Business Valuation Standards.

Steven D. Hyden, CPA, ASA is a managing director of The Financial Valuation Group (FVG) in Tampa, Florida. Mr. Hyden is also president of Hyden Capital, Inc., an affiliate firm providing merger and acquisition advisory services.

Mr. Hyden is an FCG recognized specialist for "Financial Reporting in Intangible Assets and Goodwill Impairment." He has coauthored and taught 10 valuation courses. He was guest expert for the AICPA Continuing Professional Education video course series, "Valuation of Intellectual Property."

Mr. Hyden has been a full-time business appraiser and expert witness for over 17 years, specializing in intangible assets, including intellectual property. He has developed analyses that have been reviewed and accepted by the Securities and Exchange Commission, numerous accounting firms (including the Big Five), the IRS, and the courts.

Mark L. Zyla, CPA/ABV, CFA, ASA, is a shareholder with Phillips Hitchner (PH), a financial advisory firm located in Atlanta, Georgia. Mr. Zyla has more than 15 years of financial advisory and valuation experience. He has provided financial advisory services for closely held businesses for the purposes of mergers and acquisitions, gift and estate tax planning, corporate recapitalizations, as well as many other purposes. He has also been involved in the allocation of purchase price for financial and tax reporting purposes including the valuation of such intangible assets as patents, trademarks, software, noncompete agreements, and other proprietary technology. Prior to joining PH, he was with PriceWaterhouseCoopers where he was the practice leader for Coopers & Lybrand's Corporate Finance Consulting Group for the Southeastern United States. He is also an FCG recognized specialist for "Financial Reporting in Intangible Assets and Goodwill Impairment."

Mr. Zyla is a member of the American Institute of Certified Public Accountants (AICPA), the Association for Investment Management and Research, and the Atlanta Society of Financial Analysts. Mr. Zyla is a former member of the Business Valuations Committee of the AICPA. He is a current member of the Business Valuation Committee of the Georgia Society of CPAs. He is also a member of the Atlanta Venture Forum, a professional organization of the venture capital community.

©2001. The Financial Valuation Group, L.C. Used with permission.

Chapter 1

History of Mergers and Acquisitions and Financial Reporting

The accounting rules for mergers and acquisitions changed dramatically on June 29, 2001, with the issuance by the Financial Accounting Standards Board (FASB or Board) of Statement of Financial Accounting Standards (SFAS) No. 141, *Business Combinations* and SFAS No. 142, *Goodwill and Other Intangible Assets*. Collectively, the two Statements ended pooling of interests and goodwill amortization, and substituted a framework for analyzing goodwill for impairment.

The evolution of purchase accounting rules in general, and the recognition and amortization of intangible assets in particular, were motivated by ever-increasing merger and acquisition activity in the second half of the twentieth century. Accounting rule-makers definitively addressed the issue in 1970, with the issuance of Accounting Principles Board (APB, the predecessor organization to the FASB) Opinion No. 16, *Business Combinations*. APB Opinion No. 16 provided stricter requirements for recognizing a business combination as a pooling of interests than had existed up to that point.

Purchase accounting required that the cost of an acquisition, that is, the fair value of the assets acquired in a transaction, be reflected on the books of the surviving entity. A purchase price that exceeded the fair value of the recorded assets of the enterprise meant recognizing the existence and value of acquired intangible assets and amortizing them as appropriate. Pooling of interests was an exception; then the balance sheets of combining entities were merged.

Prior to the release in 1970 of APB Opinion No. 17, *Intangible Assets*, generally accepted accounting principles (GAAP) recognized intangible assets as having either a **limited** or **indefinite** life; the former were amortized over their remaining useful lives and the latter were not amortized at all. APB Opinion No. 17 states that "the value of intangible assets at any one date eventually disappears and that the recorded costs of intangible assets should be amortized."[1] This required that *all* intangible assets be amortized over a period not to exceed 40 years.[2] With SFAS No. 142, the treatment of indefinitely lived intangible assets has come full circle.

The need for accounting rules that bring order and consistent reporting to the merger and acquisition arena has become increasingly important. The impact of mergers and acquisitions (M&A) on the economy and financial reporting is a critical issue. In recent years this need has grown dramatically. As shown in Exhibit 1.1, *Mergerstat Review*[3] reported 9,566 deals were announced in 2000 compared with 2,074 in 1990. That's an average annual increase of 16.5 percent for the 10-year period. In terms of total deal value, shown in Exhibit 1.2, the total value of the deals in 2000 was $1,325.7 billion, compared with $108.2 billion in 1990, an average annual increase of 28.5 percent. Clearly, the importance of accurate and consistent accounting for business combinations has never been greater.

Until SFAS Nos. 141 and 142 were enacted, guidelines for accounting for business combinations were codified in APB Opinion Nos. 16 and 17.

Exhibit 1.1   Net Merger and Acquisition Announcements

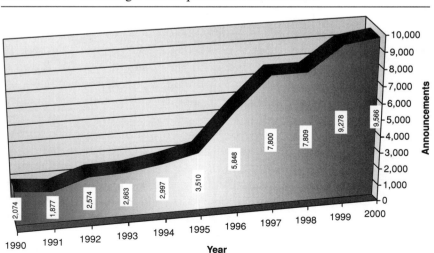

Exhibit 1.2　Total Dollar Value Offered

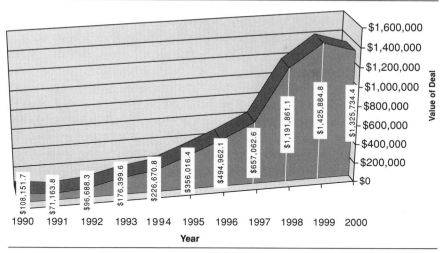

APB Opinion No. 16 recognized two distinct methods of accounting for business combinations—the *purchase* method and the *pooling of interests* method. As described in APB Opinion No. 16, "The purchase method accounts for a business combination as the acquisition of one company by another;"[4] whereas "The pooling of interests method accounts for a business combination as the uniting of the ownership interests of two or more companies by exchange of equity securities."[5]

In a purchase:

> The acquiring corporation records as its cost the acquired assets less liabilities assumed. A difference between the cost of an acquired company and the sum of the fair values of tangible and identifiable intangible assets less liabilities is recorded as goodwill. The reported income of an acquiring corporation includes the operations of the acquired company after acquisition, based on the cost to the acquiring corporation.[6]

In a pooling:

> No acquisition is recognized because the combination is accomplished without disbursing resources of the constituents. Ownership interests continue and the former bases of accounting are retained. The recorded assets and liabilities of the constituents are carried forward to the

combined corporation at their recorded amounts. Income of the combined corporation includes income of the constituents for the entire fiscal period in which the combination occurs. The reported income of the constituents for prior periods is combined and restated as income of the combined corporation.[7]

The principle distinction in the accounting treatment of a purchase compared with a pooling is that in a purchase the fair values of the assets of the acquired corporation were recorded on the books of the purchaser, while in a pooling, no step-up of assets to fair value was recognized. Further, the fair values of assets recognized under purchase accounting were subject to periodic amortization under APB Opinion No. 17.[8]

The pooling of interests method was applied only to business combinations involving the exchange of stock. Importantly, APB Opinion No. 16 set forth 12 specific conditions, all of which had to be met for a business combination to be classified as a pooling of interests:

1. Each of the combining companies must be autonomous and must not have been a subsidiary or division of another corporation during the two-year period prior to the initiation of the combination plan.
2. Each of the combining companies is independent of the other combining companies.
3. The combination is effected in a single transaction or is completed in accordance with a specific plan within one year after the plan is initiated.
4. The surviving (or resultant parent) corporation must issue *only* common stock with rights identical to those of the majority of its outstanding voting common stock, in exchange for "substantially all" (90 percent or more) of the voting common stock of the other (combining) companies outstanding.
5. Each of the combining companies must maintain substantially the same voting common stock interest.
6. The combining companies may reacquire shares of voting common stock *only* for purposes other than business combinations.
7. The ratio of the interest of an individual common stockholder to those of other common stockholders in a combining company must remain the same.
8. The voting rights of the common stock interests must be exercisable by the stockholders.

9. The combination must be resolved at the date the plan is consummated, with no pending provision of the plan relating to the issue of securities or other consideration.
10. The combined corporation must not agree directly or indirectly to retire or reacquire all or part of the common stock issued.
11. The combined corporation must not enter into other financial arrangements for the benefit of the former stockholders of a combining company.
12. The combined corporation must not intend to dispose of a significant part of the assets of the combining companies within two years after the combination, except to eliminate duplicate facilities or excess capacity and those assets that would have been disposed of in the ordinary course of business of the separate company.[9]

The pooling of interests method provided certain benefits to the merged enterprise, including no recognition of amortization charges over the life of the acquired assets. However, compliance with the 12 specific conditions severely limited deal flexibility for the merger partners.

Proponents of pooling argued:

> . . . an exchange of stock to effect a business combination is in substance a transaction between the combining stockholder groups and does not involve the corporate entities. The transaction therefore neither requires nor justifies establishing a new basis of accountability for the assets of the combined corporation. Those who endorse the purchase method believe that the transaction is an issue of stock by a corporation for consideration received from those who become stockholders by the transaction. The consideration received is established by bargaining between independent parties, and the acquiring corporation accounts for the additional assets at their bargained—that is, current—values.[10]

Arguments for purchase accounting included:

> Those who favored the purchase method of accounting believe that one corporation acquires another company in almost every business combination. . . . Proponents of purchase accounting hold that a business combination is a significant economic event, which results from bargaining between independent parties. . . . The agreed terms of combination recognize primarily the bargained values and only secondarily the costs of assets and liabilities carried by the constituents. . . . Accounting by the purchase method is essentially the same whether the business combination is effected by distributing assets, incurring liabilities, or is-

suing stock because issuing stock is considered an economic event as significant as distributing assets or incurring liabilities. . . . The purchase method adheres to traditional principles of accounting for acquisition of assets.[11]

The rules allowing the participants in a business combination to choose between two conceptually opposite accounting methods lasted 30 years, ending with SFAS No. 141.

Just as SFAS Nos. 141 and 142 interact and should be read and applied in tandem, so too were APB Opinion Nos. 16 and 17. APB Opinion No. 17 classified intangible assets as **identifiable** and **unidentifiable**. In addition, APB Opinion No. 17 mandated that intangibles be classified as having either a **limited** or **unlimited** life. Prior to this opinion, management had significant latitude in handling intangible asset amortization. APB Opinion No. 17 decreed that all intangible assets, whether identifiable or unidentifiable, must be amortized. Any intangible asset for which a remaining useful life could not be reasonably ascertained was amortized over a period not to exceed 40 years.[12] APB Opinion No. 17 also set forth a number of factors to be considered in estimating the remaining useful lives of intangible assets.[13]

HISTORY OF THE FASB DELIBERATIONS

In August 1996, the FASB announced its project to reconsider APB Opinion Nos. 16 and 17. The FASB took on the project for five main reasons:[14]

1. The Financial Accounting Standards Advisory Counsel (FASAC) had consistently urged assigning a high priority to the revisions of standards affecting business combinations, most recently at its July 1996 meeting.
2. The FASB and the Securities and Exchange Commission (SEC) were devoting increasing resources responding to inquiries from the auditing profession relating to clarification of APB Opinion Nos. 16 and 17 to specific fact situations.
3. These interpretations increasingly led to perceived flaws and deficiencies, particularly when two transactions are not significantly different, but are accounted for by methods producing dramatically different financial statement results diminishing their integrity.
4. The Board continued to recognize the need for international com-

parability of accounting standards that would enhance the movement of capital flows globally. The FASB had been working with the Australian Accounting Standards Board, The New Zealand Financial Standards Board, the United Kingdom Accounting Standards Board, the Canadian Institute of Chartered Accountants, and the International Accounting Standards Committee with the goal of achieving international convergence with respect to the methods of accounting for business combinations. As part of this cooperation, the FASB issued a position paper, *Methods of Accounting for Business Combinations: Recommendations of the G4+1 for Achieving Convergence*, on December 15, 1998. They received 267 responses.

5. The Board had come to believe that the pooling of interests method created an unlevel playing field domestically and internationally for acquirers who may or may not be able to apply that method.

Over the period of deliberation, there was much activity with many presentations invited by the FASB. Ed Jenkins, Chairman, testified before Congress on this project three times in the year 2000. Further, he participated in oversight hearings before and round table discussions held by the Senate Committee on Banking, Housing and Urban Affairs. In September 2000, the Board met with a team of representatives from the American Business Conference (including representatives from Cisco Systems, Merrill Lynch and Co., TechNet, and the United Parcel Service) to discuss a proposed impairment test that would apply to purchased goodwill. In May 2000, the Board met with a team of representatives from the investment banking community and several public accounting firms to discuss the residual income valuation model (technically known as the Multi-Period Excess Earnings Model) to measure and account for goodwill. In January 1999, the Board and staff met with representatives of the AICPA Business Valuation subcommittee, authors Michael J. Mard, CPA/ABV, ASA and James R. Hitchner, CPA/ABV, ASA for an educational meeting on identifying, valuing, and lifing purchased intangible assets. Methodologies were presented along with over 500 legal case citations in which the central issue was the valuation of intangibles. This included the U.S. Supreme Court case, *Newark Morning Ledger Co. v. U.S.*[15]

With all of this activity and the international reach created by the FASB leadership, Congress had to get into the act. On October 3, 2000, representative Christopher Cox (R-California) introduced a bill in the House of Representatives that would, if enacted, postpone proposed improvements to the transparency of business combinations.[16] The bill was ultimately opposed and the challenge to the leadership of the FASB receded.

The FASB issued its first exposure draft, *Proposed Statement of Financial Accounting Standards, Business Combinations and Intangible Assets*, on September 7, 1999. This draft called for the amortization of goodwill over a fixed 20-year period. The FASB issued a revised exposure draft, *Business Combinations and Intangible Assets— Accounting for Goodwill*, in February 2001. This revised draft called for the goodwill impairment model and the Board received over 200 comment letters.

While the Board was ferreting through these deliberations over many years, academia got into the act too. A study by professors Hopkins, Houston, and Peters entitled *Purchase, Pooling and Equity Analysts' Valuation Judgments*, concluded empirically that accounting does matter. The professors provide evidence that analysts' stock price judgments depend on the method of accounting for a business combination as well as the number of years that have elapsed since the combination. Analysts' stock price estimates are lowest when a company applies the purchase method of accounting and ratably amortizes the acquisition premium (goodwill). Time is correlated with the analysts' price estimates only when the company applies the purchase method and ratably amortizes goodwill. However, when a company uses the purchase method and writes off the acquisition premium (such as in-process research and development [IPR&D]), analysts, stock price judgments are not statistically different from their judgments applicable to a company applying a pooling of interests method. As stated by the Hopkins, Houston, and Peters study:

> The controversy over accounting for business combinations has dogged regulators and standard setters for more than half a century. The heart of the controversy centers on the noncomparable financial statements that result from the two generally accepted methods of accounting for business combinations: purchase and pooling of interests.
>
> The purchase method is consistent with the accounting rules typically applied to assets purchased in the ordinary course of business. The target's net assets are reported in the consolidated balance sheet at the fair value of the consideration (usually cash or stock) exchanged for the target's common shares. The difference between the fair value paid for the target and the book value of the target's net assets is called the ac-

counting acquisition premium (AAP). The AAP is first allocated to the fair values of the target's identifiable net assets. Any remaining (unallocated) AAP is classified as goodwill and amortized over a period not to exceed 40 years.

In contrast, pooling requires the acquirer to record the historical book values of the target's net assets. The AAP is not recorded in combinations that qualify for pooling treatment; therefore, they generally report higher net income relative to otherwise identical combinations that apply the purchase method. In addition, pooling requires the acquirer to recognize the target's net income for the entire year in which the business combination occurred, regardless of the actual transaction date. Under pooling, prior years' financial statements are restated to combine the financial statements of the two companies as if they have always been a single economic unit. This unusual mixture of book-value recognition and prior-period restatement originated almost a century ago "for combinations in which a strong degree of affiliation existed between the combining entities prior to the combination" (FASB 1998, Appendix p. 3). Since that time, this treatment has been extended to combinations of entities without prior affiliation.[17]

The impact of the accounting method on earnings per share can be dramatic and may lead to perceived distortions, not necessarily because of the method of accounting, but rather because different players are involved. As Hopkins, Houston, and Peters state:

Although the use of the purchase or pooling accounting is not a choice, *per se*, companies that otherwise would be required to use purchase accounting appear to be willing to incur significant direct and indirect costs to qualify for pooling treatment. Empirical and anecdotal evidence suggests that companies incur significant costs to meet APB 16's pooling criteria. For example, while Nathan (1988) did not find higher acquisition premia for firms applying the pooling method, Robinson and Shane (1990), David (1990), Vincent (1997), and Ayers et al. (2000a) suggest that poolings result in higher acquisition premia than purchases. Ayers et al. (2000a) estimate that 15 percent of the acquisition premium in poolings is attributable to the cost of obtaining pooling treatment. Similarly, Lys and Vincent (1995) suggest that ATT, in its acquisition of NCR, incurred approximately $50 million of incremental costs to qualify for pooling treatment.

These higher premia suggest that either fundamental differences exist between the companies that qualify for pooling versus purchase accounting, or acquirers are willing to pay an additional amount for the future accounting benefits afforded by pooling. Based on a sample of firms using the pooling method, Ayers et al. (2000b) estimated that EPS [earnings per share] would have been 18.5 percent lower, and median ROE [return on equity] and market-to-book ratios 22 percent lower, had these firms used the purchase method. Consequently, if investors do not adjust for the post-acquisition accounting differences between purchase and pooling, then structuring business combinations to qualify for pooling-of-interest treatment (and avoiding the AAP's drag on reported income) may benefit combining companies. However, if a business combination is structured as a tax-free reorganization, then application of the two methods results in identical past, present, and future direct cash flows. There, *for otherwise identical companies*, an efficient-markets perspective suggests that applying different business-combination accounting methods should *not* affect stock prices.[18] [Emphasis added]

The Hopkins, Houston, and Peters study concluded:

. . . analysts' price judgments were lowest when the company applied purchase accounting and ratably amortized goodwill. Analysts estimated higher prices when the company applied either pooling-of-interest accounting or purchase accounting with immediate write-off of the acquisition premium as in-process research and development.

The results of the timing manipulation supported our salience-based predictions. Analysts' stock price estimates were lowest when the company acquired its subsidiary *three years* before the current fiscal year, applied the purchase method, and ratably amortized goodwill. When the business combination occurred in the *most recent* fiscal year, purchase accounting with goodwill amortization resulted in stock-price judgments that were (1) higher than when the company applied the same method of accounting to a three-year-old business combination, (2) lower than each case (i.e., one year and three years after the combination) of pooling-of-interest accounting, and (3) lower than each case of purchase accounting with immediate write-off of the acquisition premium as in-process research and development. In addition, regardless of the timing of the business combination, analysts' price judgments did not statistically differ between pooling-of-interest accounting and purchase accounting with immediate write-off of the acquisition premium as in-process research and development.

. . . We extend both Hopkins (1996) and Hirst and Hopkins (1998) by demonstrating that fundamental variation in accounting method—in this case, accounting for business combinations—has a predictable effect on analysts' stock-price estimates and the amount of value-relevant net income included in their valuation models. . . . Our results suggest that analysts are more likely to remove from reported net income the effects of large, one-time charges. . . . Compared to ratable amortization that causes prolonged reduction of reported earnings, analysts are more likely to discount the effects of a non-cash charge if it is presented as a one-time item.[19]

The result of the Hopkins, Houston, and Peters study is demonstrated in Exhibit 1.3.

Exhibit 1.3 Analysts' Common Stock Price Judgments by Business-Combination Accounting Method and Business-Combination Timing Conditions[20]

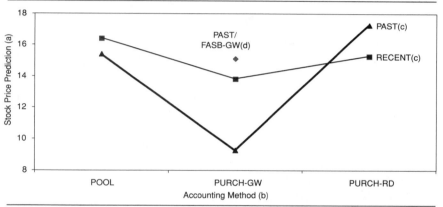

(a) Analysts estimated the price of a company's common stock (PRICE) after receiving information about the company and its industry, including an income statement, balance sheet, statement of cash flows, statement of changes in owner's equity, and a summary of significant accounting policies. We held constant all information, except the information directly related to the two independent variables.

(b) The method of accounting for the business combination varied between subjects as (1) pooling of interests ("POOL"), (2) purchase with the accounting acquisition premium (AAP) capitalized as goodwill and amortized over six years ("PURCH-GW"), or (3) purchase with the AAP expensed as in-process research and development ("PURCH-RD"). Because the business combination was consummated via a tax-free exchange of common shares, cash flows were identical across accounting methods.

(c) The business combination occurred either at the beginning of the most recent fiscal year ("RECENT") or at the beginning of the three-years-prior fiscal year ("PAST").

(d) We also constructed a set of PURCH-GW materials that incorporated the FASB's proposed reporting format for presentation of goodwill amortization (i.e., PAST/FASB-GW). Except for modifying the income statement location of goodwill (i.e., immediately preceding net income) and providing a per-share amount for pre-amortization income, the materials were identical to those presented to PAST/PURCH-GW analysts.

IMPLICATIONS

The implications of the new rules on future merger and acquisition activity are not so clear. As companies report the results of goodwill impairment testing, major write-downs will certainly result. On January 7, 2002, AOL Time Warner announced it expected to take a goodwill write-off of up to $60 billion[21] (almost half the amount recorded pursuant to the merger) as a result of impairment testing under SFAS No. 142. A look at the company's closing stock prices indicates that this news did not impact the closing price significantly:

Day	Date	Closing Price
Friday	January 4, 2002	$31.95
Monday	January 7, 2002	32.68
Tuesday	January 8, 2002	32.00

The 52-week high for AOL Time Warner stock was $58.51. At the above dates the stock was trading near its 52-week low. Thus, a devaluation of AOL Time Warner stock had already occurred in the minds of investors and the company and its accountants had decided the impairment was permanent. In other words, the economic or business dog wagged the accounting tail, as it should.

While the landscape of accounting for mergers and acquisitions has changed significantly, the effect of the rules on M&A activity is uncertain. CFO.com reports "Wall Street seems to be considering the reporting changes something of a non-event."[22] An article in *The Times* indicated analysts believe the total write-off could reach $1 trillion.[23] *The Times* further reported the statement of Bob Willens, an accounting analyst with Lehman Brothers, who said, "If you add it all up it's pretty easy to get to $1 trillion. . . . But I don't think it will have much of an effect on stocks because it is already priced into the market."[24]

While the consensus seems to be that the recognition of goodwill impairment losses will reflect rather than drive reductions in stock prices, the new accounting rules are expected to have an effect on deal activity. A case in point is the battle for control of Wachovia Corporation. Chief financial officer Robert Kelly of First Union Corporation said the new rules' framework "provides us with a lot more flexibility than pooling."[25]

The demise of pooling will allow combining companies to be more creative in structuring deals. PriceWaterhouseCoopers predicted that the disappearance of pooling will have the following impact on future deals:

- Flexibility to sell noncore assets—pooling rules contained restrictions on the disposal of acquired assets
- Increased use of cash in deals—pooling rules forbade cash consideration
- Treasury stock repurchases will become more popular—the old pooling rules restricted the reacquisition of stock
- Greater flexibility in structuring compensation programs—the pooling rules restricting a company's ability to cash out, alter, or grant new equity awards are no longer relevant
- More contingent consideration—the old pooling rules prohibited earnouts[26]

Bear Stearns has predicted:

We also expect to see an increase in M&A activity, particularly in industries that have been sensitive to earnings dilution. While not producing the same financial reporting results as a pooling, purchase accounting without goodwill amortization will greatly level the playing field for both acquirers and targets.[27]

Bear Stearns further explains:

With the elimination of pooling and its 12 criteria, there will also be more flexibility to structure transactions efficiently. Not only will companies that are, or had been, a subsidiary or a division of another company any time in the last two years become more attractive, companies will no longer be compelled to buy all or retain all of the target. In addition, it eliminates a barrier to "hostile" transactions.[28]

The following chapters explain and illustrate the accounting rules in greater detail. But what can we expect of their impact on the world that creates the need for such rules? Is there any consensus on the future effect of the two Statements on M&A activity?

As mentioned earlier, the AOL impairment example would suggest that investors are not greatly swayed by impairment charges in earnings announcements of companies that had combined under the old rules. Observers are already cautioning that, "The facts and circumstances surrounding each goodwill impairment charge will need to be evaluated for their investment significance."[29] Ms. McConnell of Bear Stearns writes:

> In the past, a goodwill impairment charge was often considered the sign of a bad acquisition, a miscalculation of the value of the target (i.e., the acquirer overpaid), or an unexpected deterioration in the fundamentals of the business acquired. Under the new rules, a goodwill impairment charge within a few years of the acquisition date may be an indication of any of these as well. However, as time goes by, it is less likely that an impairment is an indication of a bad acquisition or an overpayment. In fact, it is possible that the investment may have been recovered with an appropriate return but, because there has been no amortization, the goodwill remains on the balance sheet. A goodwill impairment many years after an acquisition is more likely to be an indication of the third condition, deterioration in the fundamentals of the business. As noted above, if the market has already anticipated this, the actual recognition of the loss will not have an additional impact on the stock price.[30]

Many think fears of a major impact are overblown. Sophisticated investors should easily grasp the earnings impact of the new pronouncements. Those who hold this view further argue that the effect of the new rules for GAAP will be blunted since more and more investors increasingly evaluate companies on measures based on cashflow or operating earnings. To the extent that earnings dilution still worries companies, the elimination of goodwill amortization charges will ease the fears of management that have been holding back from acquisitions because of the spectre of future accounting charges.

The Hopkins, Houston, and Peters study found that the accounting method did matter. But their study was completed in 1999, well before SFAS Nos. 141 and 142 were released, and acquirers still had a choice. Indeed, they had the prescience to test the proposed goodwill amortization-reporting protocol described in FASB's business combinations exposure draft.[31] When analysts were provided income statements that contained the improved disclosure, they generally provided higher stock price judgments than analysts who received income statements with traditional goodwill amortization.[32]

It does not appear that many commentators are predicting a general decline in stock prices due to the new reporting rules. It seems to be generally accepted that investors will adjust to the new reporting, especially in industries that are valued using price/earnings ratios. Investors will make the necessary adjustments to more or less maintain stock prices. On the other hand, many observers believe that the elimination of pooling and its restrictions combined with a leveling of the playing field in terms of financial reporting will actually have a positive effect on future M&A activity. No one has a crystal ball and it is safe to say that the implementation of the new rules will not be problem-free. However, SFAS Nos. 141 and 142 are law, so financial executives and their advisors must obtain a clear understanding of them.

Chapter 2

SFAS No. 141, Goodwill and Other Intangible Assets in a Business Combination

Recent changes in regulatory requirements leading to the identification and measurement of intangible assets are discussed in this chapter. We will discuss at length SFAS No. 141 and the new in-process research and development (IPR&D) Practice Aid. Chapter 3 will augment this discussion by providing a detailed example of a purchase price allocation, illustrated with the valuation of seven distinct identifiable intangible assets acquired in a business combination.

WHAT ARE INTANGIBLE ASSETS?

It seems everyone believes he knows what an intangible asset is until it comes time to actually write a precise definition. The Report of the Brookings Task Force on Intangibles (Brookings Task Force) defined intangibles as:

> . . . nonphysical factors that contribute to or are used in producing goods or providing services, or that are expected to generate future productive benefits for the individuals or firms that control the use of those factors.[1]

The International Valuation Standards Committee was, perhaps more precise in defining intangible assets as:

> . . . assets that manifest themselves by their economic properties, they do not have physical substance, they grant rights and privileges to their

owner; and usually generate income for their owner. Intangible Assets can be categorized as arising from Rights, Relationships, Grouped Intangibles, or Intellectual Property.[2]

The International Valuation Standards Committee goes on to define each category.

Probably the briefest definition was provided by the FASB:

> . . . assets (not including financial assets) that lack physical substance.[3]

Per the FASB, intangible assets are distinguished from goodwill. The FASB provides specific guidance for the identification of intangible assets such that any asset not so identified would fall into the catch-all category of goodwill.

Each of these definitions are correct and, in their venue, appropriate. But the nature of intangible assets requires more explanation. Intangible assets are a subset of human capital, which is a collection of education, experience, and skill of a company's employees. Structural capital is distinguished from human capital but also includes intangible assets such as process documentation and the organizational structure itself, which is the supportive infrastructure provided for human capital. This encourages human capital to create and leverage its knowledge. Intangible assets are the codified physical descriptions of specific knowledge that can be owned and readily traded. Separability and transferability (specific to the asset or attached to another) are fundamental prerequisites to the meaningful codification and measurement of intangible assets. Further, intangible assets receiving legal protection become intellectual property, which is generally categorized into five types: patents, copyrights, tradenames (-marks and -dress), trade secrets, and know-how.

WHY ARE INTANGIBLE ASSETS SO DIFFICULT TO MEASURE?

Traditional accounting rests on the foundation of historical cost: If there is an invoice, there is an asset and it can be measured. The corollary, however, invites ridicule: If there is no invoice, there is no asset. The Brookings Task Force was succinct regarding measurement difficulties when it said:

> Because one cannot see, or touch, or weigh intangibles, one cannot measure them directly but must instead rely on proxies, or indirect measures, to say something about their impact on some other variable that can be measured.[4]

Over the years, the FASB has sought to change the historical cost focus of measurement. In fact, the FASB has increasingly required fair value determination as applicable to specific Statements of Financial Accounting. There are approximately three dozen Statements that require consideration of fair value.[5] As of this writing, the scope of a new FASB project, "Disclosure of Information about Intangible Assets not Recognized in Financial Statements,"[6] focuses on the disclosure of internally generated intangible assets that are not recognized in financial statements. One of the authors of this book, Michael J. Mard, serves on this project's working group, which will study how the identification and measurement of internally generated intangible assets should be reported in the financial statements. Such potential reporting ranges from footnote disclosure to full financial statement disclosure.[7] Clearly, the identification and measurement of intangible assets is becoming recognized and accepted by the market. How is this done?

THE NATURE OF INTANGIBLE ASSETS

Opportunity cost is a mainstay of finance. Many finance courses focus on the opportunities available to utilize tangible assets, with the goal of applying those tangible assets to the opportunity with the highest return. Opportunities not selected can be viewed as returns foregone or opportunity cost. The physical reality is that tangible assets can only be in one place at one time. Professor Baruch Lev, New York University, Stern School of Business, looked at the physical, human, and financial assets (all considered tangible) as competing for the opportunity. In a sense, these assets are rival or scarce assets ". . . in which the scarcity is reflected by the cost of using the assets (the opportunity foregone)."[8]

Such assets distinguish themselves from intangible assets in that intangible assets do not rival each other for incremental returns. In fact, intangible assets can be applied to multiple uses for multiple returns. As Professor Lev says:

> The non-rivalry (or non-scarcity) attribute of intangibles—the ability to use such assets in simultaneous and repetitive applications without diminishing their usefulness—is a major value driver at the business enterprise level as well as at the national level. Whereas physical and financial assets can be leveraged to a limited degree by exploiting economies of scale or scope in production (a plant can be used for at most three shifts a day), the leveraging of intangibles to generate benefits—the scalability of these assets—is generally limited only by the size of the market. The usefulness of the ideas, knowledge, and research embedded in a new drug or a computer operating system is not limited by the diminishing returns to

scale typical of physical assets (as production expands from two to three shifts, returns decrease due, for example, to the wage premium paid for the third shift and to employee fatigue). In fact, intangibles are often characterized by increasing returns to scale. An investment in the development of a drug or a financial instrument (a risk-hedging mechanism, for example), is often leveraged in the development of successor drugs and financial instruments. Information is cumulative, goes the saying.[9]

IDENTIFICATION AND CLASSIFICATION

Identification of intangible assets is as broad as the business mind is creative. There are the well-accepted intangibles such as customer base, in-process research and development, and technology, as well as intellectual property such as patents, copyrights, trademarks, trade secrets, and know-how. The value of these assets typically account for a vast majority of an enterprise's total intangible value, depending on the industry. There are also unique intangible assets peculiar to an industry or enterprise such as deposits in a bank.

In an attempt to provide some structure to the recognition of identifiable intangible assets and to enhance the longevity of its financial model, the FASB has classified intangibles into five categories:

1. Marketing-related intangible assets
2. Customer-related intangible assets
3. Artistic-related intangible assets
4. Contract-based intangible assets
5. Technology-based intangible assets[10]

The FASB goes on to provide an explanation and examples for each of the categories (Exhibit 2.1).[11] Notably, assembled workforce is excluded because it fails the separability and transferability test. A company may have the best employees of the highest value in the world, but they have no value if separated from the business. Further, the Board was not confident of the reliability of the measurement tools most often used for assembled workforce and its associated intellectual capital. The FASB instead chose to categorize assembled workforce within the components of goodwill.[12] Exhibit 2.2[13] provides an expanded but unclassified list of intangibles culled from numerous tax court cases over the years and most recently presented in the AICPA's Consulting Services Practice Aid 99-2, *Valuing Intellectual Property and Calculating Infringement Damages*.

Exhibit 2.1   Examples of Intangible Assets that Meet the Criteria for Recognition Apart from Goodwill

The following are examples of intangible assets that meet the criteria for recognition as an asset apart from goodwill. The following illustrative list is not intended to be all-inclusive; thus, an acquired intangible asset might meet the recognition criteria of this Statement but not be included on that list. Assets designated by the symbol (*) are those that would be recognized apart from goodwill because they meet the contractual-legal criterion. Assets designated by the symbol (♦) do not arise from contractual or other legal rights, but shall nonetheless be recognized apart from goodwill because they meet the separability criterion. The determination of whether a specific acquired intangible asset meets the criteria in this Statement for recognition apart from goodwill shall be based on the facts and circumstances of each individual business combination.

A. Marketing-related intangible assets
  1. Trademarks, trade names *
  2. Service marks, collective marks, certification marks *
  3. Trade dress (unique color, shape, or package design) *
  4. Newspaper mastheads *
  5. Noncompetition agreements *
B. Customer-related intangible assets
  1. Customer lists ♦
  2. Order or production backlog *
  3. Customer contracts and the related customer relationships *
  4. Noncontractual customer relationships ♦
C. Artistic-related intangible assets
  1. Plays, operas, and ballets *
  2. Books, magazines, newspapers, and other literary works *
  3. Musical works such as compositions, song lyrics, advertising jingles *
  4. Pictures and photographs *
  5. Video and audiovisual material, including motion pictures, music videos, and television programs *
D. Contract-based intangible assets
  1. Licensing, royalty, standstill agreements *
  2. Advertising, construction, management, service or supply contracts *
  3. Lease agreements *
  4. Construction permits *
  5. Franchise agreements *
  6. Operating and broadcast rights *
  7. Use rights such as landing, drilling, water, air, mineral, timber cutting, route authorities, and so forth *
  8. Servicing contracts such as mortgage servicing contracts *
  9. Employment contracts *
E. Technology-based intangible assets
  1. Patented technology *
  2. Computer software and mask works *
  3. Internet domain names *
  4. Unpatented technology ♦
  5. Databases, including title plants ♦
  6. Trade secrets including secret formulas, processes, recipes *

Exhibit 2.2 These are identifiable and transferable, have a determinate life, and may not be subject to the day-to-day work efforts of the owner.

- Airport gates and slots
- Bank customers, including deposits, loans, trusts, and credit cards
- Blueprints
- Book libraries
- Brand names
- Broadcast licenses
- Buy–sell agreements
- Certificates of need
- Chemical formulas
- Computer software
- Computerized databases
- Contracts
- Cooperative agreements
- Copyrights
- Credit information files
- Customer contracts
- Customer and client lists
- Customer relationships
- Designs and drawings
- Development rights
- Distribution networks
- Distribution rights
- Drilling rights
- Easements
- Employment contracts
- Engineering drawings
- Environmental rights
- FCC licenses
- Favorable financing
- Favorable leases
- Film libraries
- Food flavorings and recipes

- Franchise agreements
- Historical documents
- HMO enrollment lists
- Insurance expirations
- Insurance in force
- Joint ventures
- Know-how
- Laboratory notebooks
- Landing rights
- Leasehold interests
- Literary works
- Loan portfolios
- Location value
- Management contracts
- Manual databases
- Manuscripts
- Medical charts and records
- Mineral rights
- Musical compositions
- Natural resources
- Newspaper morgue files
- Noncompete covenants
- Options, warrants, grants, rights
- Patent applications
- Patents (both product and process)
- Patterns
- Permits
- Prescription drug files
- Prizes and awards
- Procedural manuals
- Production backlogs

- Product designs
- Property use rights
- Proposals outstanding
- Proprietary computer software
- Proprietary processes
- Proprietary products
- Proprietary technology
- Publications
- Retail shelf space
- Royalty agreements
- Schematics and diagrams
- Securities portfolios
- Security interests
- Shareholder agreements
- Solicitation rights
- Stock and bond instruments
- Subscription lists
- Supplier contracts
- Technical and specialty libraries
- Technical documentation
- Technology-sharing agreements
- Title plants
- Trade secrets
- Trained and assembled workforce
- Trademarks and trade names
- Training manuals
- Use rights (air, water, and land)

THE MEASUREMENT OF INTANGIBLE ASSETS

The International Valuation Standards (IVS) Guidance Note No. 6, *Business Valuation*, addresses factors to be considered in valuing intangible assets.[14] Further, in its delineation of applicable methodology, IVS Guidance Note No. 6 provides the basic economic approaches (the cost approach, the income approach, and the market approach) to valuing intangible assets.[15]

A key fundamental underlying the valuation of intangible assets is the concept of the tension between risk and return. As Professor Lev states:

> Assuredly, all investments and assets are risky in an uncertain business environment. Yet the riskiness of intangibles is, in general, substantially higher than that of physical and even financial assets. For one, the prospects of a total loss common to many innovative activities, such as a new drug development or an internet initiative, are very rare for physical or financial assets. Even highly risky physical projects, such as commercial property, rarely end up as a loss. . . . A comparative study of the uncertainty associated with R&D and that of property, plant, and equipment confirms the large risk differentials: the earnings volatility (a measurement of risk) associated with R&D is, on average, three times larger than the earnings volatility associated with physical investment.[16]

A fundamental tenet of economics holds that return requirements increase as risk increases with intangible assets inherently more risky than tangible assets. It is reasonable to conclude that the returns expected on intangible assets typically will be at or above the average rate of return (discount rate) for the company as a whole. The relationship of the amount of return, the rate of return (including risk), and the value of the asset creates a mathematical formula used in analysis (see Exhibit 2.3).

The following sections discuss recent regulatory changes affecting intangible assets and goodwill including the standard of value.

FAIR VALUE AND BUSINESS COMBINATIONS

The definition of fair value as stated in SFAS No. 141 is:

> The amount at which that asset (or liability) could be bought (or incurred) or sold (or settled) in a current transaction between willing parties, that is, other than in a forced or liquidation sale.[17]

Exhibit 2.3 The income approach is heavily relied on when valuing intangibles. Typically, two of three elements are known or can be computed, thus leading to a solution for the third.

If	$\dfrac{\$ \text{Return}}{\text{Rate of Return}}$	=	Value for Intangible Asset
Then	$\dfrac{\$ \text{Return}}{\text{Value}}$	=	Rate of Return
And	$\dfrac{\text{Rate of Return}}{\text{Value}} \times$	=	\$ Return

In contrast, fair *market* value is defined in the Internal Revenue Code as:

> The price at which the property would change hands between a willing buyer and a willing seller when the former is not under any compulsion to buy and the latter is not under any compulsion to sell, both parties having reasonable knowledge of relevant facts.[18]

A principal difference between the two definitions is that fair value for the business enterprise considers synergies and attributes of the specific buyer and specific seller (i.e., the purchase price of the business combination), while fair market value contemplates a hypothetical willing buyer and a hypothetical willing seller. These issues are discussed in more detail later in the chapter.

A business combination occurs when an enterprise acquires net assets that constitute a business or equity interest of one or more enterprises and obtains control over that enterprise or enterprises.[19] Though there are certain exceptions, such as the acquisition of an equity interest held by minority shareholders and acquisitions of not-for-profit organizations, all business combinations as defined by the Statement should be accounted for using the purchase method of accounting. In SFAS No. 141, the use of the pooling of interests method was immediately prohibited. Application of the purchase method requires identification of all assets of the acquiring enterprise, both tangible and intangible.[20] Any excess of the cost of an acquired entity over the net amounts assigned to the tangible and intangible assets acquired and liabilities assumed will be classified as goodwill.[21]

RECOGNITION OF INTANGIBLE ASSETS

As stated earlier, the definition of intangible assets includes current and noncurrent assets (not including financial instruments) that lack physical substance.[22] An acquired intangible asset shall be recognized apart from goodwill if that asset arises from contractual or other legal rights. If an intangible asset does not arise from contractual or other legal rights, it shall be recognized apart from goodwill only if it is separable. That is, it must be capable of being separated or divided from the acquired enterprise and sold, transferred, licensed, rented, or exchanged (regardless of whether there is an intent to do so). An intangible asset that cannot be sold, transferred, licensed, rented, or exchanged individually is still considered separable if it can be paired with a related contract, asset or liability and sold, transferred, licensed, rented, or exchanged. An important exception to the individual recognition of intangible assets is the value of an assembled workforce of "at will" employees. Thus, a group of employees acquired in a business combination who are not bound by an employment agreement will be recorded as goodwill regardless of whether the asset meets the criteria for recognition apart from goodwill.[23]

Residual value should factor into determining the amount of an intangible asset to be amortized and is defined as the estimated fair value of an intangible asset at the end of its useful life less any disposal costs. A recognized intangible asset with an indefinite useful life may not be amortized until its life is determined to be no longer indefinite. If no legal, regulatory, contractual, competitive, economic, or other factors limit the useful life of an intangible asset, the useful life of that asset should be considered indefinite. The term *indefinite* does not mean infinite. A recognized intangible asset that is not amortized must be tested for impairment annually, and on an interim basis if an event or circumstance occurring between annual tests indicates that the asset might be impaired.[24]

TAX EFFECTS

Intangible assets are valued after tax. Tax effects include providing for income taxes in any forecast of cash flow, providing for tax amortization of intangible assets over a 15-year period per Internal Revenue Code Section 197. Fair value should also capture "amortization benefit," that is, the incremental value attributable to an intangible by virtue of its tax deductibility. Including the tax effects in the valuation process is common in the income and cost approaches, but not typical in the market approach, since any tax effect is routinely factored into the quoted market price (such as the price to net earnings multiple).

CONTRIBUTORY CHARGES (RETURNS ON AND OF)

Imbedded in the concept that the fair value of an identifiable intangible asset is equal to the present value of the net cash flows attributable to that asset is the notion that the net cash flows attributable to the subject asset must recognize the support of many other assets, tangible and intangible, which contribute to the realization of the cash flows. The *contributory asset charges* (of cash flow) are based on the fair value of the contributing assets. After-tax cash flows for certain identifiable intangible assets are assessed charges representing a "return on" and a "return of" the contributory assets based on their fair values. The *return on* the asset refers to a hypothetical assumption whereby the project pays the owner of the contributory assets a fair return on the fair value of the hypothetically rented assets (in other words, return on is the payment for using the asset). For self-developed assets (such as assembled workforce or customer base), the cost to replace these assets is already factored into the cash flow analysis as part of the operating cost structure in the form of ongoing development expenses. Similarly, the return of fixed assets is included in the cost structure as depreciation. *Return of* is the cost to replace the asset and is deducted from the subject revenues (see Exhibit 2.4).

PRESENT VALUE CONSIDERATIONS FOR INTANGIBLE ASSETS

The FASB concludes that fair value is the objective when using present value in measurements at the initial recognition and fresh-start measurements of assets. Two approaches are specifically recognized: the expected cash flow approach and the traditional approach.[25] The expected cash flow approach focuses on the variations in the amount and timing of estimated cash flows and their relative probability of occurrence. The traditional approach attempts to capture those same factors by focusing on

Exhibit 2.4   A company's tangible and intangible rates of return can be presented as:

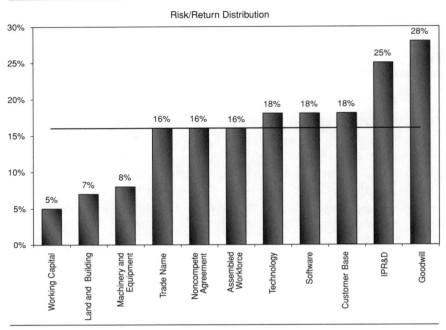

Where:
1. The midline of the distribution represents the company's discount rate,
2. Items below the midline represent returns on tangible assets (such as working capital: 5% and land and buildings: 7%),
3. Items above the midline represent returns on intangible assets (such as IPR&D: 25% and customer base: 18%), and
4. The highest rate of return represents the riskiest asset, goodwill.
© 2002. The Financial Valuation Group, LC. Used with permission.

the selection of an interest rate that is commensurate with the risk. The Statement notes five elements of a present value measurement, which taken together capture the economic differences among assets:

1. An estimate of the future cash flow, or in more complex cases, series of future cash flows at different times
2. Expectations about possible variations in the amount or timing of those cash flows
3. The time value of money, represented by the risk-free rate of interest
4. The price for bearing the uncertainty inherent in the asset or liability

5. Other, sometimes unidentifiable, factors including illiquidity and market imperfections[26]

Estimates of future cash flows are subject to a variety of risks and uncertainties, especially related to new product launches, such as:

- The time to bring the product to market
- The market and customer acceptance
- The viability of the technology
- Regulatory approval
- Competitor response
- The price and performance characteristics of the product[27]

The risk premium assessed in a discount rate should decrease as a project successfully proceeds through its continuum of development, since the uncertainty about accomplishing the necessary first step and each subsequent step diminishes.

IN-PROCESS RESEARCH AND DEVELOPMENT

In this technological age, as research and development (R&D) activities become an increasingly larger part of industrial activity, the financial reporting of assets to be used in R&D activities, especially specific in-process research and development (IPR&D) projects, has become increasingly controversial.

Acquired IPR&D is particularly prevalent in the pharmaceutical, software, and devices industries. The subject of IPR&D has been comprehensively addressed in the AICPA Practice Aid Series, *Assets Acquired in a Business Combination to Be Used in Research and Development Activities: A Focus on Software, Electronic Devices, and Pharmaceutical Industries* (the IPR&D Practice Aid). The IPR&D Practice Aid states, "This Practice Aid identifies what the Task Force members perceive as best practices related to defining and accounting for, disclosing, valuing, and auditing assets acquired to be used in R&D activities, including specific IPR&D projects."[28] Those readers wishing a more detailed analysis of the subject should refer to the IPR&D Practice Aid.

In-process research and development can be generally defined as a research and development project that has not yet been completed.

Acquired IPR&D is a subset of an intangible asset to be used in R&D activities. Costs to be allocated to assets acquired to be used in R&D activities should possess the characteristics of control and expected economic benefit, with fair value being estimable with reasonable reliability. If an asset to be used in R&D activities is a specific IPR&D project, that project should have both substance and be incomplete.[29]

SFAS No. 2, *Accounting for Research and Development Costs*, defines R&D and sets forth broad guidelines as to the activities that constitute R&D activities. Assets to be used in R&D activities subsequently are accounted for under FASB Interpretation No. 4, *Applicability of SFAS No. 2 to Business Combinations Accounted for by the Purchase Method*. GAAP generally requires that the fair value of acquired IPR&D be immediately charged to income, but may be amortized if an alternative future use exists for the asset. Separately identifiable assets include both tangible and intangible assets.

An acquiring company's interest in such assets is controllable by the combined enterprise such that it can obtain benefit from the asset and control others' access to the asset. Acquired IPR&D has economic benefit when the acquiring company can demonstrate that each such asset, either singly or in combination with other assets, will be used in postcombination R&D activities.[30]

The IPR&D Practice Aid is consistent with FASB Statement of Financial Accounting Concepts 6, *Elements of Financial Statements*, which states:

> Assets are probable future economic benefits obtained or controlled by a particular entity as a result of past transactions or events. . . . An asset has three essential characteristics: (a) it embodies a probable future economic benefit that involves a capacity, singly or in combination with other assets, to contribute directly or indirectly to future net cash flows, (b) a particular entity can obtain the benefit and control others' access to it, and (c) the transaction or other event giving rise to the entity's right to or control of the benefit has already occurred.[31]

Examples of control include:

- The combined enterprise has the ability to sell, lease, license, franchise, or use its rights to the R&D asset acquired; or
- The combined enterprise has proprietary intellectual property rights, which it believes could be successfully defended if its ownership were challenged.[32]

The fair value of acquired IPR&D must be measurable, that is, it must be able to be estimated with reasonable reliability. The economic benefit of the product, service, or process that is expected from the IPR&D effort must be sufficiently determinable such that a reasonably reliable estimate of the future expected net cash flows can be made based on assumptions that are verifiable. For example, a reasonably reliable estimate of fair value may be determinable if the following seven components of IPR&D can be estimated with confidence:

1. A market for the product
2. Time needed to commercialize and market the product
3. Potential customers and market penetration
4. The effects of competitors' existing or potential products
5. The combined enterprise's share of the market
6. The selling price
7. Production and related costs for the product[33]

The basic form of an IPR&D life cycle will at some point lead to the acquiring company likely being able to estimate fair value with reasonable reliability. This basic form includes:

- *Conceptualization*, which is an idea, thought, or plan for a new product and includes an initial assessment of the potential market, cost, and technical issues for such concepts.
- *Applied research*, which is the planned search or critical investigation aimed at the discovery of new knowledge including assessing the feasibility of successfully completing the project.
- *Development*, which translates the research into a detailed plan or design for a new product, service, or process.
- *Preproduction*, which represents the business activities necessary to commercialize the asset.[34]

To be recognized as an asset, specific IPR&D projects must have substance, which is the recognition of sufficient cost and effort that would enable the project's fair value to be estimated with reasonable reliability.[35] Further, the IPR&D must be incomplete in that there are remaining technological, engineering, or regulatory risks.[36]

Recommended financial statement disclosure includes but is not limited to the identification of the following by the acquiring company:

- A description of the projects to which value was ascribed, including the status of the project
- The values assigned to each of the assets acquired including the amount of the in-process R&D charge
- The techniques used in each acquisition to value assets acquired to be used in R&D activities
- The key assumptions used in valuing the assets acquired to be used in R&D activities, such as:
  a. The time frame for cash flows expected to be realized, and
  b. The weighted average discount rates used in determining present values[37]

Cost should be assigned to all identifiable tangible and intangible assets, including any resulting from R&D activities of the acquired company or to be used in R&D activities of the combined enterprise. The acquiring company should allocate a portion of the purchase price to each acquired identifiable intangible asset that possesses either of the following characteristics:

- Produces cash flows that are largely independent of cash flows generated by other assets
- Could realistically be licensed, sold, transferred, exchanged or disposed of in a transaction in which it is the only asset.[38]

For the purpose of valuation, cash flows should be allocated to each intangible asset on an as-if-separated basis, representing the typical cash flow carve-outs and returns on and of charges in the multiperiod excess earnings model. Importantly, synergistic value may not be attributed to an acquired identifiable asset. Thus, synergistic value falls into goodwill, which is calculated on a residual basis. As stated in the IPR&D Practice Aid:

> A willing buyer may factor into the amount that it would pay to acquire the seller's business a portion of the incremental cash flows that are expected to inure to the benefit of that buyer. The incremental cash flows may include those resulting from strategic or synergistic components. If the buyer pays the seller any significant consideration for strategic or synergistic benefits in excess of those expected to be realized by market participants, the valuation specialist would identify those excess benefits and remove them from the valuation of assets acquired. Thus, the cost of the acquired company may include an element of

synergistic value (i.e., investment value). However, for purposes of assigning cost to the assets acquired in accordance with FASB Statement No. 141, the amount of the purchase price allocated to an acquired asset would not include any entity-specific synergistic value. Fair value does not include strategic or synergistic value resulting from expectations about future events that are specific to a particular buyer because the value associated with those components is unique to the buyer and seller and would not reflect market-based assumptions. Therefore, entity-specific value associated with strategic or synergistic components would be included in goodwill. Fair value would incorporate expectations about future events that affect market participants. If the acquiring company concludes that the discounted cash flow method best approximates the fair value of an acquired asset, the discounted cash flows would incorporate assumptions that market participants would use in their estimates of fair values, future revenues, future expenses, and discount rates (if applicable).[39]

Although the determination of fair value revolves around the three classic approaches to valuation, cost, market, and income, the relief from royalties method and the multiperiod excess earnings method are particularly relied on.

The analyst should review certain information in order to properly evaluate management's identification and classification of assets acquired (including IPR&D intangibles). At a minimum, this would include:

- Presentations to the board of directors
- Offering memoranda
- Due diligence reports
- Press releases (both of the acquiring and the acquired companies)
- Web site materials
- Analysts reports
- Industry reports[40]

Prospective Financial Information (PFI) is provided by management, but the sources, methodologies, procedures, adjustments, and application must be tested by the analyst. The IPR&D Practice Aid states:

> . . . PFI provided by management that is accepted by the valuation specialist without having been subjected to validating procedures by the valuation specialist would contradict the performance of best practices. . . .[41]

Further, the IPR&D Practice Aid states:

> The valuation specialist does not simply accept PFI from management without investigating its suitability for use in the valuation analysis. The valuation specialist is responsible for evaluating the methodology and assumptions used by management in preparing the PFI and concluding whether the PFI is appropriate for use in valuing the assets acquired.[42]

As stated above, the analyst should determine and document that a particular R&D project has substance. In addition to the consideration of the information reviewed to properly evaluate management's identification and classification of assets acquired, the basis for such documentation should include:

- Stage of completion of the project
- Treatment and emphasis given to the project in the company's product road-map for the technology
- Acquired company's R&D budget
- Acquired company's R&D planning documents and related status reports
- R&D costs incurred by project and estimated costs to complete the project[43]

Further, the analyst must conclude that the R&D project is incomplete as of the acquisition date based on the following:

- Stage of development as indicated by the development milestones attained and yet to be reached
- Remaining technological, engineering, or regulatory risks to be overcome
- Remaining development costs to be incurred
- Remaining time to be spent to reach completion
- Probability of successful completion[44]

Finally, the analyst should conclude and document whether the assets acquired to be used in R&D activities have an alternative future use. If so, the value of that asset would be capitalized and amortized pursuant to SFAS Nos. 141 and 142. If the assets acquired to be used in R&D activities do not have an alternative use, those costs would be charged to expense as of the date of acquisition.[45]

Appendix 2.1

INTELLECTUAL PROPERTY

One of the major difficulties in valuing intellectual property is determining the context of licensor/licensee negotiations. All too often this context is assumed or simplified, resulting in market royalty rates being applied out of context. Most valuation analysts traditionally develop royalty rates from three traditional sources:

1. Negotiated licensing agreements
2. Surveys performed by various professionals, generally in cooperation with trade associations
3. Judicial opinions, which vary greatly depending on individual fact patterns

These traditional tools can now be augmented by databases of licensing agreements extracted from publicly available sources. Such direct market data is some of the most compelling evidence available to determine the appropriate royalty rate in a valuation.

The market comparison–transaction method approach is used to value intellectual property. This approach initially has four steps to derive an overall value estimate: (1) **research** the appropriate market for comparable intellectual property transactions; (2) **verify** the information by confirming that the market data obtained is factually accurate and that the license exchange transactions reflect arm's-length market considerations; (3) **compare and apply** the guideline license transactions' financial and operational aspects to the subject intellectual property; and (4) **reconcile** the various value indications into a single value indication or range of values.

EMPIRICAL RESEARCH AND VERIFICATION OF ROYALTY RATES

Proprietary research of intangible assets and intellectual properties is important in business valuation. The value the market perceives in intellectual property-intensive companies is associated with their intangible assets and intellectual properties. Valuation of such companies is often an exercise in intangible asset valuation methods rather than traditional business valuation methods. Emphasis should be placed on proprietary studies (industry research, industry pricing metrics, and comparable intellectual property transactions). Research and verification of comparable data can be a time-consuming process. Recently, advances in information technology and the availability of online public records have made research of intellectual property transactions a realistic endeavor.

Databases that gather and organize comparative intellectual property transactions are rapidly becoming the tool of the future to those analysts who specialize in intellectual property valuation. At the time of publication, there are three known Internet sites that have collated data or provide information for a fee:

- RoyaltySource (www.royaltysource.com)
- Consor® (www.consor.com)
- The Financial Valuation Group (www.fvginternational.com)

COMPARING AND APPLYING THE DATA

Intellectual property transactions should be compared to the subject company using the following guidelines:

- The specific legal rights of intellectual property ownership conveyed in the guideline transaction
- The existence of any special financing terms or other arrangements
- Whether the elements of arm's length existed for the sale or license conditions
- The economic conditions that existed in the appropriate secondary market at the time of the sale or license transaction
- The industry in which the guideline intellectual property was or will be used
- The financial and operational characteristics of the guideline properties, compared with the subject company's intellectual property

RECONCILIATION

The last phase of the market approach valuation analysis is the reconciliation. The strengths and weaknesses of each comparable transaction are considered; the reliability and appropriateness of the market data examined, including the analytical techniques applied. After considerable re-view, transactions selected should be reasonably comparative to the company and then synthesized into a reasonable range.

DETAILED EXAMPLE OF AN INTELLECTUAL PROPERTY DATABASE

The intellectual property transactions database of The Financial Valuation Group is based on publicly available data. It includes approximately 40 fields comprised of the names of the licensor and licensee, both the Standard Industrial Classification (SIC) and North American Industry Classification System (NAICS) numbers for the licensor and the licensee, the type of agreement (i.e., trademark, patent, copyright), the industry name, the remuneration structure, royalty percentages (base rate, the low end and high end of variable rates), royalty dollars (base flat fee, annual and variable fees), a description of the product or service, and so on. Custom searches of the database (using keywords, SIC/NAICS numbers, or both) can be performed to obtain market comparables.

Transactions by Industry

Industry groups as represented by the first two digits of the U.S. government SIC codes are represented in transactions in the database as shown in Exhibit 2.5.

Exhibit 2.5   Intellectual Property Transactions Database by Two-Digit SIC Industry

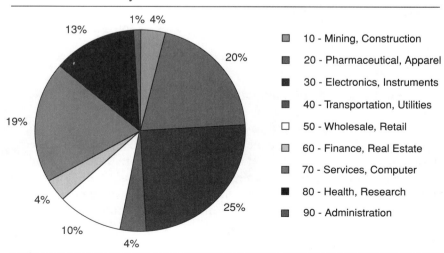

□ 10 - Mining, Construction
■ 20 - Pharmaceutical, Apparel
■ 30 - Electronics, Instruments
▨ 40 - Transportation, Utilities
□ 50 - Wholesale, Retail
▨ 60 - Finance, Real Estate
▨ 70 - Services, Computer
■ 80 - Health, Research
▨ 90 - Administration

Exhibit 2.6   Database Percentages for Intellectual Property Types

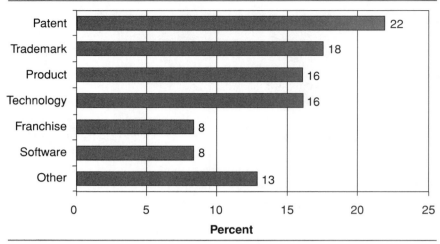

Intellectual Property Typically Licensed

While there are approximately 90 distinctly different intangible assets, the majority of assets licensed are intellectual property assets which can be grouped as shown in Exhibit 2.6.

Patents tend to be the most-licensed intellectual property, with trademarks, products, and technology following respectively.

Payment Structures of Intellectual Property Transactions

A comparison of the royalty payment structures disclosed in each transaction reveals that approximately half of the licensing agreements are based on a set percentage or set dollar amount. There are many transactions that involve high/low payments, which are usually based on performance, sales, or both. Annual Fee and Monthly Fee agreements tend to be set at a fixed amount paid on a regular basis throughout the life of the agreement. Exhibit 2.7 shows the various royalty rate payment structures by the reported transactions analyzed.

Exhibit 2.7 Payment Structure of Database Transactions

Legend	Slice
Fixed Dollars and Fixed Percent Combined	
Fixed Percent	
Percent Variable	
Percent and Dollar Combined, Variable	
Dollar Variable	
Fixed Dollars	
Royalty Fee	
Undisclosed/Unknown	

Pie chart values: 25%, 14%, 7%, 4%, 25%, 8%, 5%, 12%

Reasons to Use the Database

The database is used to support:

- Damages in an intellectual property litigation case
- Reasonable royalty percentage rates
- Accurate valuation conclusions
- Rebuttal of unreasonable value estimates put forth by others
- Transfer pricing opinions

Because royalty rates derived from transactions take so many economic structures, it is difficult to interpret them in a manner that is useful for a particular need. Analysis of licensing transactions similar to a particular fact situation would be necessary to determine a market royalty rate applicable to that situation. The analyst with requisite skill, education, and experience will be able to draw upon the data to form well-founded and defensible conclusions and opinions.

Determining Goodwill and Other Intangible Assets in a Business Combination: A Case Study

Under generally accepted accounting principles (GAAP), an acquiring company must record the fair value of the assets acquired in a business combination. SFAS No. 141 mandates such purchase accounting for all acquisitions.[1] At face value, purchase accounting is a simple process—determine the total purchase price paid for an entity and allocate that purchase price to the various assets acquired. However, the valuation of intangibles is more complex. This section presents an example of a purchase price allocation.

There are numerous complexities in a purchase price allocation and there are various challenges to be met along the way. These challenges include:

- Determining the purchase price—the purchase price is more than just the cash and/or publicly traded stock paid for an acquisition; notes issued and/or liabilities assumed increase the purchase price. Contingent considerations muddy the waters (e.g., contingent events, earnouts, restricted or nonmarketable securities tendered, etc.).
- Performing a valuation of the acquirer to determine the value of its stock if the purchase price includes the payment of stock of a privately held acquirer.
- Identifying all acquired assets, tangible and intangible.
- Identifying if the sum of the fair values of the assets may exceed the purchase price.

- Dealing with situations where data for valuing or estimating the useful life of certain assets may be limited or not available.

The example presented in the following pages is of an acquisition of the *assets* of a *privately held* corporation, and may differ in the treatment of certain issues compared with an acquisition of stock or public company acquisition. While the numerous steps and processes are presented sequentially, in reality the various activities are performed simultaneously over a period of weeks, often by a staff of several analysts.

SFAS No. 141 states that the cost of an acquired entity should be measured with reference to cash payments, fair values of other assets distributed as consideration, and the fair values of liabilities incurred by an acquiring entity.[2] This *adjusted* purchase price may be alternatively defined as the sum of all cash and stock paid, debt incurred, and liabilities assumed. In this example, the adjusted purchase price is assumed to be $209,000,000 based on the following assumptions:

Cash paid*	$150,000,000
Liabilities assumed	
Current liabilities**	25,000,000
Current maturities of long-term debt	4,000,000
Long-term debt	30,000,000
Adjusted purchase price	$209,000,000

*Including capitalized acquisition costs
**Excluding externally funded debt

As used here, the term *adjusted purchase price* equals the total paid for all of the acquired company's assets, and includes all payments and liabilities assumed. It is important to distinguish this measurement from the concept of *invested capital*, which is defined as the sum of debt and equity in an enterprise on a long-term basis,[3] shown here as $184,000,000.

At this point, it is useful for the analyst to understand the overall magnitude of the intangible assets. This can be easily achieved by subtracting from the adjusted purchase price (or total asset value) the estimated fair value of the current and tangible assets. An analysis of the company's balance sheet and asset records as of the valuation date reveals the recorded or carrying value of the assets is $67,500,000, which consists of:

	Carrying Value
Cash	$ 1,500,000
Marketable securities	4,000,000
Accounts receivable	17,000,000
Inventory	12,000,000
Prepaid expenses	3,000,000
Land and building	10,000,000
Machinery and equipment	15,000,000
Organization costs and	
other intangibles	5,000,000
Total current and tangible assets	$67,500,000

The next step is to adjust recorded values to fair values, including final audited amounts if available. In reality, separate valuations may be undertaken of material tangible assets. For example, a machinery and equipment appraiser may be brought in to independently value the fixed assets if it is determined that (a) the fixed assets are material, and (b) the book values do not represent fair value. Similarly, the valued receivables and other current assets may not be reflected by their carrying value and require adjustment to fair value. For purposes of this analysis, it is assumed that adjustments are required to certain asset accounts. After the adjustments, the fair values of the tangible assets are:

	Carrying Value	**Fair Value**
Cash	$ 1,500,000	$ 1,500,000
Marketable securities	4,000,000	8,000,000[a]
Accounts receivable	17,000,000	17,000,000
Inventory	12,000,000	12,000,000
Prepaid expenses	3,000,000	3,000,000
Land and building	10,000,000	22,000,000[b]
Machinery and equipment	15,000,000	19,000,000[c]
Organization costs and		
other intangibles	5,000,000	0[d]
Total current and tangible assets	$67,500,000	$82,500,000

a. Fair value of marketable securities, as marked to market.
b. Fair value per real estate appraisal.
c. Fair value per machinery and equipment appraisal.
d. Written off (see "Valuation of Current Assets" section later in this chapter).

The fair value of the tangible assets is $82,500,000, so the "gap" available for all intangible assets is $126,500,000 ($209,000,000 − $82,500,000). As a picture is worth a thousand words, the foregoing relationship is illustrated by a "box analysis." Exhibits 3.1 and 3.2 set forth the general allocation formula according to the box analysis, where the left side of the exhibit represents the asset side of the balance sheet, and the right represents the liabilities and equity section of the balance sheet.

The assumed values of the various categories of assets, liabilities, and equity are shown in Exhibit 3.2. The box analysis is quite useful, especially when presented with complex purchase arrangements. Note that while current maturities of long-term debt are usually classified as current liabilities for accounting purposes, this debt is included with the

Exhibit 3.1   General Allocation Formula

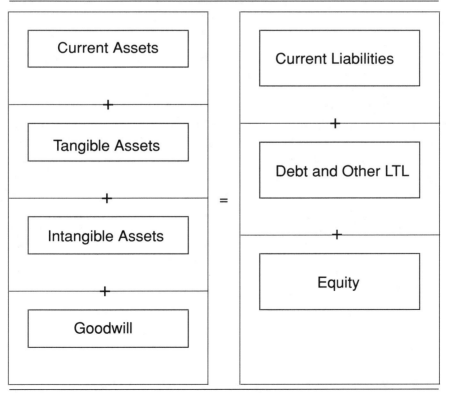

Exhibit 3.2   General Allocation Formula

$209,000,000	Current Assets $41,500,000	=	Current Liabilities $25,000,000	$209,000,000
	+		+	
	Tangible Assets $41,000,000		Debt and Other LTL (including short-term portion) $34,000,000	
	+		+	
	Intangible Assets and Goodwill $126,500,000		Equity $150,000,000	

© 2002. The Financial Valuation Group, LC. Used with permission.

long-term portion in our valuation analysis because it represents part of the total invested capital in the business.

In our example, the adjusted purchase price (cash paid plus liabilities assumed) is $209,000,000. By referring to Exhibit 3.2, it should be easily seen that this equates to a total asset value of $209,000,000 and that the total of intangible assets and goodwill is $126,500,000.

Data gathering and management interviews are critical. Assume that an investigation of the target and its operations has been conducted and it has been determined that there are seven intangible assets that are identifiable and are subject to being valued. At this point, the methodologies to be used to value the intangibles are fairly clear, although the valuation and allocation process is fluid and changes in methods and approaches may be made as the engagement proceeds. The intangibles and the approach or method to be used are set forth in the following table.

Asset	Type	Valuation Approach (Method)
Software	Technology-based	Cost approach (cost to recreate)
Customer relationships	Customer-related	Cost approach (cost to recreate)

Assembled workforce[4]	Goodwill	Cost approach (cost to recreate)
Noncompete agreement	Contract-based	Income approach (before and after DCF)
Technology	Technology-based	Income approach (multi-period excess earnings)
In-process research and development	Technology-based	Income approach (multiperiod excess earnings)
Trade name	Marketing-related	Income approach (relief from royalties)
Goodwill	N/A	Residual

The valuation of the purchased assets of Target Company will be performed using a combination of cost and income approaches, with an element of the market approach in selecting the royalty rate used in the trade name valuation. Detailed explanations of the three approaches are beyond the scope of this book but may be found in various valuation texts. The multiperiod excess earnings method of the income approach will be used to value technology and in-process research and development (IPR&D). However, the other assets must be valued first (aside from goodwill, which is valued using a residual method, where the value of all identified assets is subtracted from the total adjusted purchase price). This is because one of the inputs of the multiperiod excess earnings method is a deduction representing returns or contributory charges on the fair values of the other assets employed in the business.

REMAINING USEFUL LIFE ANALYSIS

Identifiable assets must be analyzed to determine whether the asset has a finite or indefinite useful life. This subject is addressed in SFAS No. 142:

> The accounting for a recognized intangible asset is based on its useful life to the reporting entity. An intangible asset with a finite useful life is amortized; an intangible asset with an indefinite useful life is not amortized. The useful life of an intangible asset to an entity is the period over which the asset is expected to contribute directly or indirectly to the future cash flows of that entity.[5]

SFAS No. 142 mentions a number of pertinent factors that should be taken into account:[6]

- Expected use of the asset
- Expected use of similar assets
- Legal, regulatory, and contractual provisions that may limit the useful life or enable renewal or extension
- The effects of obsolescence, demand, competition, and other economic factors
- Required future maintenance expenditures

Analysts also rely on statistically based predictions of future behavior by developing *survivor curves* using tools such as Iowa-type curves and the Weibull Distribution. The subject of "lifing" is very complex and beyond the scope of this book. There is no shortage of writings on the topic; for a start, Chapter 11 of *Valuing Intangible Assets* by Robert F. Reilly and Robert P. Schweihs (New York: McGraw-Hill, 1999) is recommended.

In the following example, it is assumed that various analyses and techniques have been performed to determine the remaining useful lives of the amortizable intangible assets, but those machinations will not be described.

BUSINESS ENTERPRISE VALUE

Our analysis will proceed with the development of a business enterprise valuation (BEV) using a discounted cash flow (DCF) methodology. Performing the BEV using a DCF requires a number of assumptions including: sales and expense forecasts, working capital requirements, and capital expenditure requirements. The nature and underlying rationale for these assumptions will be discussed throughout the chapter.

In this example, the adjusted purchase price comprises invested capital (as previously defined) plus current liabilities. The adjusted purchase price is equivalent to current assets plus tangible assets, intangible assets, and goodwill. The value of a business enterprise is equivalent to the value of the total invested capital of that business. A company's invested capital is equivalent to net working capital (determined by deducting the amount of current liabilities from current assets) plus tangible assets, intangible assets, and goodwill. Again, the box analysis is helpful (see Exhibit 3.3).

Performing a BEV and DCF are important in three major respects.

Exhibit 3.3 Target Company Business Enterprise Analysis-Assumptions as of December 31, 2001

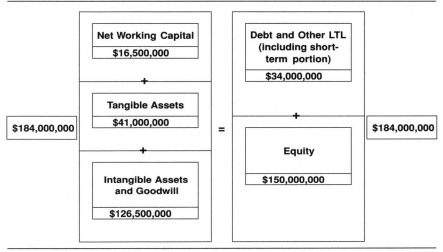

© 2002. The Financial Valuation Group. Used with permission.

First, it requires an in-depth review of the industry and of Target Company's operations and results, both historical and forecasted. Second, it allows the analyst to ascertain the reasonableness of the purchase price by determining whether the expected future cash flows of an enterprise will support that purchase price. Third, in performing a BEV, revenue, earnings, and cash flow streams are forecast, which serve as the basis for valuing assets by the income approach.

DISCOUNTED CASH FLOW METHOD

In the discounted cash flow method of the income approach, a pro forma analysis is made of the subject company to estimate future available cash flows. Available cash flow is the amount that can be paid out to providers of capital without impairment of business operations.

The annual forecasted available cash flows are then discounted to indicate a present value. The sum of the annual present values including the present value of any estimated residual equals the capitalized earnings value of the business. When performed on a debt-free basis, that is, assuming the company has no financial leverage, the business's capitalized earnings value equates to invested capital value, defined as the sum of equity value plus the value of all interest-bearing debt.

Assumptions should generally be prepared by the client. The analyst might guide a client to producing a meaningful forecast, but, just as historical financial statements are the responsibility of management, not the auditor, the company should take responsibility for prospective financial information (defined as a forecast of expected future cash flows, or PFI).[7] Assumptions were made on the basis of internal company PFI as presented to us. Amounts also forecast are: sales growth, product cost, operating expenses, and depreciation. As shown in Exhibit 3.4, principal assumptions utilized in developing the estimates of cash flow are:

- Sales are forecast to increase from $60,000,000 in 2001 to $69,000,000 in 2002, growth of 15 percent, due to conversions, upgrades, new customers, and price increases. This increase is based largely on estimated growth in one of its key markets of 20 percent. However, the growth rate of the key market is expected to decline after 2003. The 10-year compound annual growth rate is 9.96 percent.

- Cost of sales (40 percent of sales in 2002, improving to 39 percent thereafter) and operating expenses (30 percent in 2002, improving to 29 percent thereafter) excluding depreciation (tax basis—separately forecast using IRS MACRS tables) and amortization are also forecast. The PFI is in line with Target Company's historical averages and with management's expectations at the time of the acquisition, and were felt to represent the best estimate of these costs. These assumptions are also in line with growth rates and margins expected by similar products from similar companies in the marketplace.

- Working capital requirements (debt free) were forecast at 15 percent of sales, based on the company's historical working capital position, expected needs, and industry benchmarks.

- Capital expenditures are forecast at 1 percent of net sales. This level of capital expenditures is considered adequate to support future levels of sales.

- Tax amortization of total intangible asset value is based on Section 197 of the Internal Revenue Code, which provides for such amortization over a 15-year period.[8] The amortization acts as a tax shield and is added back to cash flow. Annual amortization is $8,433,000 ($126,500,000 ÷ 15, rounded). The reader should note that this example is of an *asset* purchase. In a *stock* purchase, the intangible assets generally would not be amortizable for tax purposes.

Exhibit 3.4 Target Company—Business Enterprise Value—Assumptions as of December 31, 2001 ($'000s)

	ACTUAL 2001	FORECAST 2002	2003	2004	2005	2006	2007	2008	2009	2010	2011
1. SALES											
Sales Growth Percentage		15.0%	15.0%	12.5%	10.0%	10.0%	7.5%	7.5%	7.5%	7.5%	7.5%
Net Sales	$60,000	$69,000	$79,350	$89,269	$98,196	$108,015	$116,116	$124,825	$134,187	$144,251	$155,070
2. EXPENSES											
Cost of Sales	$24,000	$27,600	$30,947	$34,815	$38,296	$42,126	$45,285	$48,682	$52,333	$56,258	$60,477
Cost of Sales Percentage	40.0%	40.0%	39.0%	39.0%	39.0%	39.0%	39.0%	39.0%	39.0%	39.0%	39.0%
Operating Expenses	$18,000	$20,700	$23,012	$25,888	$28,477	$31,324	$33,674	$36,199	$38,914	$41,833	$44,970
Operating Expenses Percentage	30.0%	30.0%	29.0%	29.0%	29.0%	29.0%	29.0%	29.0%	29.0%	29.0%	29.0%
Depreciation (MACRS)	$1,750	$3,097	$5,171	$3,961	$3,120	$2,544	$2,649	$2,762	$2,011	$1,246	$1,551
Other Income (Expense), net	0.0%	0.0%	0.0%	0.0%	0.0%	0.0%	0.0%	0.0%	0.0%	0.0%	0.0%
3. CASH FLOW											
Capital Expenditures		$690	$794	$893	$982	$1,080	$1,161	$1,248	$1,342	$1,443	$1,551
Capital Expenditures Percentage		1.0%	1.0%	1.0%	1.0%	1.0%	1.0%	1.0%	1.0%	1.0%	1.0%
Projected Working Capital as Percent of Sales		15.0%	15.0%	15.0%	15.0%	15.0%	15.0%	15.0%	15.0%	15.0%	1.50%
Projected Working Capital Balance (1)	$16,500	$10,350	$11,903	$13,390	$14,729	$16,202	$17,417	$18,724	$20,128	$21,638	$23,260
Projected Working Capital Requirement		(6,150)	1,553	1,488	1,339	1,473	1,215	1,306	1,404	1,510	1,623
4. OTHER											
Effective Tax Rate	40.0%	40.0%	40.0%	40.0%	40.0%	40.0%	40.0%	40.0%	40.0%	40.0%	40.0%
Required Rate of Return	16.0%										

AMORTIZATION OF INTANGIBLES (TAX)

Assumption: Intangibles receive 15-year tax life per Sec. 197

Purchase Price	$150,000
Plus: Liabilities Assumed	59,000
Adjusted Purchase Price	$209,000
Less: Tangible Assets	(82,500)
Amortizable Intangible Assets	$126,500
Divide: Tax Life (years)	15
Annual Amortization, Rounded	$8,433

(1) Balance at December 31, 2001 stated at fair value

Note: Some amounts may not foot due to rounding.

Other assumptions:

Required rate of return (discount rate)*	16.00%
Residual perpetual growth rate	5.00%
Tax rate	40.00%

*Discussed more fully in the next section, entitled "Discount Rate."

Assumptions are summarized in Exhibit 3.4, which presents the PFI for a period of 10 years.

Cash flows in year 11 are increased by the residual growth rate and then capitalized into perpetuity by dividing by the capitalization rate, defined as the difference between the discount rate and the residual growth rate. This residual value was then discounted to present value to provide the net present value of the residual cash flow. The residual cash flow represents the anticipated cash flow for years 11 to perpetuity.

Since the Section 197 amortization has a finite amortization period of 15 years, the residual calculation must be adjusted so the amortization is not capitalized into perpetuity. First, the tax benefit of the amortization of $3,373,000 (amortization of $8,433,000 multiplied by the tax rate of 40 percent, rounded) is added back to year 11 cash flow. Thus, cash flow to be capitalized ignores any amortization benefit after year 10. Then, the present value of the remaining five years of tax amortization is added to the residual calculation. This amount is $2,697,000. After the adjustments, the amortization of intangibles reflects a benefit period of 15 years.

The present value of the net cash flows, plus the present value of the residual, provides the total capitalized cash flow. The BEV is presented in Exhibit 3.5.

DISCOUNT RATE

The appropriate rate of return for valuing the enterprise is the weighted average cost of capital, the weighted average of the return on equity capital, and the return on debt capital. The weights represent percentages of debt to total capital and equity to total capital. The rate of return on debt capital is adjusted to reflect the fact that interest payments are tax deductible to the corporation.

Exhibit 3.5 Target Company—Business Enterprise Value—Cash Flow Forecast as of December 31, 2001 ($'000s)

	ACTUAL 2001	2002	2003	2004	2005	2006	2007	2008	2009	2010	2011
							FORECAST				
Sales Growth Percentage		15.0%	15.0%	12.5%	10.0%	10.0%	7.5%	7.5%	7.5%	7.5%	7.5%
Net Sales	$60,000	$69,000	$79,350	$89,269	$98,196	$108,015	$116,116	$124,825	$134,187	$144,251	$155,070
Cost of Sales	24,000	27,600	30,947	34,815	38,296	42,126	45,285	48,682	52,333	56,258	60,477
Gross Profit	36,000	41,400	48,404	54,454	59,899	65,889	70,831	76,143	81,854	87,993	94,593
Operating Expenses	18,000	20,700	23,012	25,888	28,477	31,324	33,674	36,199	38,914	41,833	44,970
Depreciation (MACRS)	1,750	3,097	5,171	3,961	3,120	2,544	2,649	2,762	2,011	1,246	1,551
Amortization of Intangibles (Tax)	0	8,433	8,433	8,433	8,433	8,433	8,433	8,433	8,433	8,433	8,433
Total Operating Expenses	19,750	32,230	36,615	38,282	40,030	42,302	44,756	47,395	49,358	51,512	54,955
Taxable Income	16,250	9,170	11,788	16,171	19,870	23,587	26,075	28,749	32,496	36,481	39,638
Income Taxes	6,500	3,668	4,715	6,469	7,948	9,435	10,430	11,499	12,998	14,593	15,855
Net Income	$9,750	$5,502	$7,073	$9,703	$11,922	$14,152	$15,645	$17,249	$19,497	$21,889	$23,783
Net Cash Flow											
Net Income		$5,502	$7,073	$9,703	$11,922	$14,152	$15,645	$17,249	$19,497	$21,889	$23,783
Capital Expenditures		(690)	(794)	(893)	(982)	(1,080)	(1,161)	(1,248)	(1,342)	(1,443)	(1,551)
Change in Working Capital		6,150	(1,553)	(1,488)	(1,339)	(1,473)	(1,215)	(1,306)	(1,404)	(1,510)	(1,623)
Depreciation		3,097	5,171	3,961	3,120	2,544	2,649	2,762	2,011	1,246	1,551
Amortization of Intangibles (Tax)		8,433	8,433	8,433	8,433	8,433	8,433	8,433	8,433	8,433	8,433
Net Cash Flow		22,492	18,331	19,717	21,154	22,577	24,351	25,890	27,195	28,616	30,594
Present Value Factor, where Discount Rate –16.0%		0.9285	0.8004	0.6900	0.5948	0.5128	0.4421	0.3811	0.3285	0.2832	0.2441
Present Value of Net Cash Flow		$20,883	$14,672	$13,605	$12,583	$11,577	$10,764	$9,866	$8,934	$8,104	$7,469

2011 Cash Flow $30,594
Less: Tax Benefit of Amortization (3,373)
2011 Cash Flow, net of Benefit $27,220

2012 Cash Flow, Assuming Growth of 5.0% $28,581
Residual Capitalization Rate 11.00%

Residual Value, 2012 $259,830
Present Value Factor 0.2441

Fair Value of Residual $63,436

Net Present Value of Net Cash Flow, **2002–2011** $118,459
Net Present Value of Residual Cash Flow 63,436
Present Value of Amortization Tax Benefit, 2012–2016 2,697

Total Invested Capital, Rounded $185,000

Amortization of Intangibles (Pretax)	2012	2013	2014	2015	2016
	$8,433	$8,433	$8,433	$8,433	$8,433
Tax Benefit of Amortization	3,373	3,373	3,373	3,373	3,373
Present Value Factor	0.2105	0.1814	0.1564	0.1348	0.1162
Present Value of Tax Benefit	$710	$612	$528	$455	$392
Sum = Fair Value of Tax Benefit	$2,697				

Note: Some amounts may not foot due to rounding.

The weighted average cost of capital is expressed in the following formula:

$$WACC = (k_e \times W_e) + (k_p \times W_p) + (k_{d(pt)}[1 - t] \times W_d)$$

Where: WACC = Weighted average cost of capital

k_e = Cost of common equity capital

W_e = Percentage of common equity in the capital structure, at market value

k_p = Cost of preferred equity

W_p = Percentage of preferred equity in the capital structure, at market value

$k_{d(pt)}$ = Cost of debt (pretax)

t = Tax rate

W_d = Percentage of debt in the capital structure, at market value[9]

The weighted average cost of capital represents the average rate of return investors require to induce them to supply all forms of long-term capital (debt and equity) to a company.

It is beyond the scope of this book to provide a detailed explanation of rates of return, and the reader is encouraged to seek reference books or other sources that provide detailed explanations of rates of return.[10] Assume an equity discount rate (which in a corporate acquisition is often calculated using the Capital Asset Pricing Model) of 20 percent and a pretax cost of debt of 6.50 percent. Further, assume a capital structure of 25 percent debt and 75 percent equity. Theoretically, an "optimal" capital structure should be used to estimate a company's WACC in the case of an acquisition. Analysts typically rely on the capital structures of public companies as a proxy for "optimal." A target capital structure of approximately 25 percent debt and 75 percent equity was estimated for Target Company, based on a review of publicly traded companies. Target Company has no preferred equity. Substituting these values into the WACC formula described previously provides the following:

$$
\begin{aligned}
WACC &= (20.00\% \times 75.00\%) + (6.50\%[1-40.00\%] \times 25.00\%) \\
&= (15.00\%) + (3.90\% \times 25.00\%) \\
&= 15.00\% + 0.97\% \\
&= 15.97\%
\end{aligned}
$$

Rounded to 16%

Applying the Cost of Capital to cash flows estimated earlier indicates the fair value of the invested capital of the target company was

$185,000,000 on the valuation date (see Exhibit 3.5). Actual invested capital is $184,000,000 (cash paid plus interest-bearing debt assumed, including current maturities), so we are confident that the discounted cash flow model reasonably reflects the value of the business and that the discount rate is reasonable as well.

VALUATION OF CURRENT ASSETS

It is very important that the valuation analyst and the auditor have open lines of communication. Certain financial and other current assets are the province of the auditor and the purchase price allocation must rely in part on audit conclusions for certain assets, such as cash and receivables. Marketable securities must be marked to market, often by simply obtaining brokerage statements. Previously recognized intangibles that represent capitalized historic expenditures, such as organization costs, are typically written off. The actual cash flow associated with these assets occurred in the past and these assets typically cannot be separated or sold apart from the acquired entity as required under SFAS No. 141. Any other previously recorded intangible value is subsumed in the current purchase price allocation and is to be reallocated.

VALUATION OF TANGIBLE ASSETS

Few valuation analysts have the experience and training to operate outside their discipline to render valuation opinions on fixed assets. If material and/or complicated, the real estate and personal property must be independently appraised. In this example, it is assumed that a real estate appraiser determined the fair value of the land and improvements to be $22,000,000 and a personal property appraiser determined the value of the machinery and equipment to be $19,000,000.

VALUATION OF INTANGIBLE ASSETS

Discount Rates

For each asset valued in the following sections a discount rate must be selected. For assets valued using the income approach, the discount rate is used to reduce future benefit streams to present value. For those assets and for assets valued using the cost approach, the discount rate is an important input for calculating the amortization benefit (see "Discount Rate" section earlier in this chapter). That rate was employed in approximating the purchase price in the BEV and also for those assets judged to be about as risky overall as the business (trade name and noncompete agreement). Discount rates for the other intangible assets were selected based on our judgment of relative risk and approximate rates of returns investors in the subject assets might require. For example, the IPR&D is incomplete and commercially unproven. Competitors likely are developing their own technologies, that will compete. Thus, the rate of return on this asset is substantially higher than the WACC.

The rates of return on the other intangibles are similarly selected with reference to the WACC. The rates for the intangible assets are:

Software	18%
Customer base	18%
Assembled workforce	16%
Trade name	16%
Noncompete agreement	16%
Existing technology	18%
In-process research and development	25%

Software

Target Company employs a sophisticated array of computer programs to manage its product and production processes (Exhibit 3.6). All product software was developed in-house and is not commercially available. A cost approach was applied to value the software, as this asset is a supporting or contributory asset with no directly attributable revenue or income streams. However, if a revenue or income stream could be attributed to this asset, and if the software had salable commercial applications, an income approach would have been considered, as that approach is often used in the valuation of software.

The company's software system comprises 20 modules, each made up of a number of programs written in C++ programming language. To apply this form of the cost approach, it is necessary to obtain a reliable indication of the cost to recreate the program. A line count (a management report detailing the number of lines of code per program and/or module) was obtained.

Next, it is necessary to determine the productivity with which the hypothetical recreation effort would take place. Here, management assessed a productivity rating of 1 to 3, noting that software rated 1 could be programmed at four lines of code per hour; software rated at 2 could be programmed at three lines of code per hour; and software rated 3, the most complex and difficult, could be programmed at two lines of code per hour. The coding rates encompass completely debugged program statements including requirements definition, systems design, debugging and documentation, testing, and so forth. In performing this purchase price allocation, it was fortunate that management had maintained detailed records of programmer productivity and supplied their metrics for such development activity.

By dividing the lines of code for each module by the coding rate, the number of hours to recreate was developed, totaling 112,507 hours for the entire system. The sum of hours was then multiplied by the blended hourly rate of $119 per hour.

In estimating the hourly rate, it was hypothesized that if the software were to be recreated today, a project team of 10 individuals would have to be assembled. The team would include one project manager, two systems analysts, one technical writer, four programmers, and two support persons. Using their fully burdened rates, the weighted average rate was calculated for the team at $119 per hour. These rates include employee benefits, facilities and overhead charges, and approximate the rates that would be charged by a software consulting firm.

Reproduction cost of the software system was determined by multiplying the total number of hours to recreate by the blended hourly rate. *Reproduction cost* is defined as:

> . . . the estimated cost to construct, at current prices as of the date of the analysis, an exact duplicate or replica of the subject intangible asset, using the same materials, production standards, design, layout, and quality of workmanship as the subject intangible asset. The reproduction intangible asset will include the same inadequacies, superadequacies, and obsolescence as the subject intangible asset.[11]

In this example, reproduction cost totals $13,388,333. Since reproduction cost equates to brand-new software, an obsolescence factor is applied to recognize the fact that the acquired software is not brand-new. Rather, it may have redundant or extraneous code and likely has been patched over the years and contains other inefficiencies that brand-new software presumably would not have. For this application, after discussing the capabilities of the software with management, it was estimated that an obsolescence factor of 25 percent was warranted, reducing the reproduction cost to its *replacement cost* of $10,041,250.

Replacement cost is defined as:

> . . . the estimated cost to construct, at current prices as of the date of the analysis, an intangible asset with equivalent utility to the subject intangible, using modern materials, production standards, design, layout, and quality of workmanship. The replacement intangible asset will exclude all curable inadequacies, superadequacies, and obsolescence that are present in the subject intangible asset.[12]

Replacement cost is then adjusted for taxes to recognize the deductibility of such expenses. The after-tax value is $6,024,750.

Amortization Benefit

Added to the after-tax value is an amortization benefit, which reflects the additional value accruing to the asset brought about by the ability to deduct the amortization of the asset over its 15-year tax life. The amortization benefit is an element of the fair value of all intangible assets that are deductible for tax purposes.

The formula for the amortization benefit is:

$$AB = PVCF \times [n/(n - \{[PV(Dr,n,-1) \times (1 + Dr)^{0.5}] \times T\}) - 1]$$

Where:

$$AB = \text{Amortization benefit}$$
$$PVCF = \text{Present value of cash flows from the asset}$$
$$n = \text{15-year amortization period}$$
$$Dr = \text{Asset specific discount rate}$$
$$PV(Dr,n,-1) \times (1 + Dr)^{0.5} = \text{Present value of an annuity of \$1 over 15 years, at the discount rate}$$
$$T = \text{Tax rate}$$

Based on the cost approach, and after adjusting for taxes and amortization benefit, it was concluded that the fair value of the software as of December 31, 2001 was $7,070,000 (rounded) (Exhibit 3.6). The remaining useful life is four years.

Exhibit 3.6 Target Company—Valuation of Acquired Software as of December 31, 2001

All software was developed internally by Company for its own use. Rights to software were transferred at acquisition.

The software is written in C++ programming language.

Valuation is based on cost to replace less obsolescence. Costs are based on internally developed Company metrics for software development productivity.

Source: Leonard Riles, Director of Product Development

IN PLACE	LINES OF CODE	PRODUCTIVITY RATING (1)	RATE (1)	HOURS TO RECREATE
Module 1	26,400	2	3.0	8,800
Module 2	32,600	3	2.0	16,300
Module 3	46,000	1	4.0	11,500
Module 4	8,480	3	2.0	4,240
Module 5	12,000	3	2.0	6,000
Module 6	12,500	2	3.0	4,167
Module 7	2,000	2	3.0	667
Module 8	32,000	2	3.0	10,667
Module 9	3,000	2	3.0	1,000
Module 10	3,000	2	3.0	1,000
Module 11	3,000	2	3.0	1,000
Module 12	13,000	2	3.0	4,333
Module 13	6,000	2	3.0	2,000
Module 14	10,000	2	3.0	3,333
Module 15	5,000	2	3.0	1,667
Module 16	6,000	2	3.0	2,000
Module 17	5,000	3	2.0	2,500
Module 18	8,000	1	4.0	2,000
Module 19	7,000	2	3.0	2,333
Module 20	54,000	3	2.0	27,000

Total Number of Lines	294,980			
Total Number of Hours to Recreate				112,507
Times: Blended Hourly Rate (see below)				$119
Reproduction Cost				$13,388,333
Less: Obsolescence (2)			25.0%	(3,347,083)
Replacement Cost				$10,041,250
Less: Taxes @			40.0%	(4,016,500)
After Tax Value Before Amortization Benefit				$6,024,750
Amortization Benefit				
Discount Rate			18.0%	
Tax Rate			40.0%	
Tax Amortization Period			15	
Amortization Benefit				1,042,321
Fair Value of Software, Rounded				**$7,070,000**

(1) Lines of code per hour, based on productivity assessment for average module of programming.
(2) Estimate based on number of lines of redundant/extraneous code and effective age and remaining economic lives of system.

SOFTWARE DEVELOPMENT COSTS - ESTIMATED PROJECT TEAM

FUNCTION	NUMBER	BURDENED HOURLY RATE
Project Manager	1	$200.00
Systems Analyst	2	150.00
Technical Writer	1	125.00
Programmer	4	115.00
Support	2	50.00
Blended Hourly Rate, Rounded		$119.00

Note: Some amounts may not foot due to rounding.

Customer Base

The company sells virtually all of its products through a network of distributors and large and midsize retail outlets. Many of these customers have done business with the company for a number of years of uninterrupted service. As part of the acquisition of Target Company, the buyer acquired this customer base and avoided the cost of having to build a customer base through years of expenditures. One measure of the value of the customer base is represented by the sales and marketing costs avoided, and the cost approach was selected as the valuation approach to value this asset, as shown in Exhibit 3.7. In many cases, the valuation of a customer base is performed using a form of income approach known as the multiperiod excess earnings method. This method is generally reserved for the intangibles with the most direct relationship to the revenue and cash flow streams. In this company, revenues are driven primarily by the technology, both existing and in-process, and the multiperiod excess earnings approach was used to value those assets.

Valuation of a Customer Base: Cost versus Income

Valuation of a customer base using the cost approach requires the identification of the selling costs associated with the generation of new customers. In this example, management indicated that the split in selling costs was roughly equivalent to the revenue split between new and existing customers. Thus, the valuation is based on that split. Depending on the nature of the business, this split between new and existing customers may vary greatly. Thus, the valuation analyst will need to appropriately identify the costs associated with generating the new customers. This is probably most easily done based on an allocation of the sales team's time, such as 40 percent spent on finding new customers, 60 percent to handle existing ones. Or, there may be certain sales or marketing people or departments that are devoted entirely to servicing existing accounts, while others spend all of their time finding new ones. In such cases, the costs can be broken out on a departmental or individual level. For many smaller businesses, top executives also spend a large amount of time in the generation of new customers, so these costs must also be considered in the analysis.

Use of the cost approach also assumes that the customers and selling effort required to obtain them are all relatively equivalent. If the company has a few customers that make up the majority of its business, then the cost approach may not be appropriate to determine the value of the customer base.

It should be noted that the income approach is often recommended for valuing a customer base. For many consumer products and "old economy" businesses, the customer relationship may have much higher value than the technology associated with the products being sold, since these products are often a commodity or near commodity that may be easily substituted with products from another vendor. The customer relationship may allow the sale of multiple products and services through the same sales channels. An income approach may be more appropriate in these cases.

To estimate the replacement cost of the customer base, total selling costs for the years ended December 31, 1999 to December 31, 2001 were calculated, based on internally prepared financial statements and sales department detail. In each year, the percentage of time and thus expenses from prospecting for new customers was determined. This percentage was applied to the company's total selling costs for each year to determine total new customer selling costs. These expenses were $123,246 in 2001, $119,938 in 2000, and $216,221 in 1999, for a total of $459,405 for the three years, during which 13 new customers were obtained. The total after-tax selling costs were $275,643, or $21,203 per customer, determined by dividing after-tax selling costs by the 13 new customers obtained during the period. Multiplying the replacement cost per new customer times the total of 261 customers in the acquired customer base provides a replacement cost of the customer base of $5,533,983. No obsolescence is recognized for this asset. The amortization benefit is $957,415. Thus, the fair value of the customer base as of December 31, 2001 was $6,490,000 (rounded) (Exhibit 3.7). The remaining useful life is five years.

Assembled Workforce

The buyer of Target Company obtained an assembled and trained workforce. Considerable expenditures for recruiting, selecting, and training would be required to replace these employees with individuals of comparable skills and expertise. By acquiring fully trained personnel, the buyer avoided the expenditures associated with hiring and training equivalent personnel. The value of the assembled workforce is represented by the assemblage cost avoided. Therefore, the cost approach is the most applicable valuation approach to value this asset. Using this approach, the costs associated with employee recruitment, selection, and training provide the measurement of value.

Exhibit 3.7   Target Company—Valuation of Customer Base as of December 31, 2001

HISTORICAL CUSTOMER DATA

YEAR	TOTAL SELLING COSTS	PERCENT OF REVENUE FROM NEW CUSTOMERS	NEW CUSTOMER SELLING COSTS	NUMBER OF NEW CUSTOMERS
2001	$5,010,000	2.46%	$123,246	4
2000	5,307,000	2.26%	119,938	5
1999	4,848,000	4.46%	216,221	4
	$15,165,000		$459,405	13

CALCULATION OF FAIR VALUE

Total Pretax Selling Costs - New Customers		$459,405
Less: Taxes @	40.0%	(183,762)
After Tax Selling Costs - New Customers		$275,643
Divide by: Number of New Customers, 1999—2001		13
Replacement Cost per New Customer		$21,203
Times: Number of Acquired Customers		261
Replacement Cost of Customer Base		$5,533,983
Amortization Benefit		
Discount Rate	18.0%	
Tax Rate	40.0%	
Tax Amortization Period	15	
Amortization Benefit		957,415
Fair Value of Customer Base, Rounded		$6,490,000

Note: Some amounts may not foot due to rounding.

Recruiting costs are incurred to obtain a new employee, who may be either untrained or previously trained. The major components of recruiting costs are employment agencies, advertising, and other recruitment-related expenses. In order to hire most professional level employees with similar skill-sets, an employment agency may be used, which would typically charge a fee based on the starting salary. For the level of employees employed by the company, the average recruiting cost is 27.5 percent of starting salary.

Training costs are incurred to train employees and bring them to the level of performance normally expected from an individual in a given position. The training costs of an employee reflect the amount of time inefficiently used by a new employee (inefficiency training cost) and the time inefficiently used by a training supervisor (direct training cost) during the first few months on the job. Training and supervisory costs were estimated by multiplying the fully burdened weekly salary of the employee by the average amount of inefficiency incurred during the training period. The inefficiency estimate used here for training and supervisory costs is 33.3 percent, or one-third of the time. This can vary depending on the business. Interview costs are estimated based on average hours per employee class, as follows:

Class	Hours
1	5
2	10
3	20

The average fully burdened interview rate is $75.00 per hour.

The summation of the hiring and training costs results in the total cost to replace the assembled workforce are summarized in Exhibit 3.8. Based on the cost approach, and after adjusting for taxes at 40 percent and adding the amortization benefit, the fair value of the assembled workforce is estimated to be approximately $1,790,000 (rounded) at December 31, 2001. No obsolescence is recognized for this asset.

SFAS No. 141 specifically prohibits the recognition of assembled workforce as an intangible asset apart from goodwill.[13] However, in the application of the multiperiod excess earnings method, which is used to value the company's existing technology and in-process research and development, contributory charges are taken on the fair values of all of the contributory assets acquired in the acquisition. The value of the assembled workforce is calculated so that a contributory charge of that asset may be taken. However, its fair value is included in goodwill in the final allocation of purchase price and is not separately represented.

Trade Name

In this example, Target Company has one valuable trade name. However, a company may have many trademarks/trade names, some with indefinite lives and some with finite lives. Depending on the purpose and scope of the valuation, each name or mark may be valued separately.

All of the company's products and services are sold under the X trade name and each major product is identified by this trade name. Upon acquiring Target Company's assets, the buyer gained and paid for the right to use this trade name. The name valued in this section enjoys great recognition and prestige in Target Company's markets. The trade

Exhibit 3.8   Target Company—Valuation of Assembled Workforce as of December 31, 2001

NO.	JOB TITLE	SALARY	20% BENEFITS	TOTAL	TRAIN. PER. CL.	YRS.	33.3% COST	27.5% RECRUIT.	INTERVIEW & H.R.	TOTAL
1	Member of Technical Staff	$90,000	$18,000	$108,000	1	0.125	$4,500	$24,750	$375	$29,625
2	Member of Technical Staff	80,250	16,050	96,300	2	0.375	12,038	22,069	750	34,857
3	Member of Technical Staff	60,000	12,000	72,000	2	0.375	9,000	16,500	750	26,250
4	Member of Technical Staff	44,953	8,991	53,944	1	0.125	2,248	12,362	375	14,985
5	Member of Operations Staff	71,641	14,328	85,969	1	0.125	3,582	19,701	375	23,658
6	Account Executive	91,170	18,234	109,404	1	0.125	4,559	25,072	375	30,006
7	Member of Technical Staff	107,888	21,578	129,466	2	0.375	16,183	29,669	750	46,602
8	Member of Technical Staff	33,244	6,649	39,893	1	0.125	1,662	9,142	375	11,179
9	Vice President	142,000	28,400	170,400	2	0.375	21,300	39,050	750	61,100
10	Member of Technical Staff	83,647	16,729	100,376	2	0.375	12,547	23,003	750	36,300
11	Member of Operations Staff	104,700	20,940	125,640	1	0.125	5,235	28,793	375	34,403
12	Chief Architect	155,500	31,100	186,600	3	0.750	46,650	42,763	1,500	90,913
13	Director of Development	135,000	27,000	162,000	2	0.375	20,250	37,125	750	58,125
14	Member of Technical Staff	77,772	15,554	93,326	2	0.375	11,666	21,387	750	33,803
15	Account Executive	94,950	18,990	113,940	1	0.125	4,748	26,111	375	31,234
16	Member of Technical Staff	81,300	16,260	97,560	1	0.125	4,065	22,358	375	26,798
17	Chief Executive Officer	250,000	50,000	300,000	1	0.125	12,500	68,750	375	81,625
18	Member of Marketing Staff	99,000	19,800	118,800	1	0.125	4,950	27,225	375	32,550
19	Member of Technical Staff	82,000	16,400	98,400	2	0.375	12,300	22,550	750	35,600
20	Member of Operations Staff	57,460	11,492	68,952	1	0.125	2,873	15,802	375	19,050
21	Account Executive	106,400	21,280	127,680	2	0.375	15,960	29,260	750	45,970
22	Member of Technical Staff	107,867	21,573	129,440	2	0.375	16,180	29,663	750	46,593
23	Member of Technical Staff	110,000	22,000	132,000	3	0.750	33,000	30,250	1,500	64,750
24	Vice President of American Sales	135,000	27,000	162,000	2	0.375	20,250	37,125	750	58,125
25	Member of Technical Staff	71,892	14,378	86,270	2	0.375	10,784	19,770	750	31,304
26	Member of Technical Staff	96,343	19,269	115,612	2	0.375	14,451	26,494	750	41,695
27	Member of Technical Staff	114,500	22,900	137,400	1	0.125	5,725	31,488	375	37,588
28	Member of Technical Staff	47,028	9,406	56,434	1	0.125	2,351	12,933	375	15,659
29	Account Executive	90,660	18,132	108,792	1	0.125	4,533	24,932	375	29,840
30	Member of Technical Staff	63,329	12,666	75,995	1	0.125	3,166	17,415	375	20,956
31	Member of Operations Staff	131,000	26,200	157,200	1	0.125	6,550	36,025	375	42,950
32	Chief Financial Officer	150,000	30,000	180,000	1	0.125	7,500	41,250	375	49,125
33	Member of Technical Staff	100,210	20,042	120,252	2	0.375	15,032	27,558	750	43,340
34	Member of Technical Staff	87,372	17,474	104,846	2	0.375	13,106	24,027	750	37,883
35	Member of Technical Staff	108,000	21,600	129,600	2	0.375	16,200	29,700	750	46,650
36	Member of Technical Staff - Nonexempt	22,326	4,465	26,791	1	0.125	1,116	6,140	375	7,631
37	Member of Technical Staff	70,000	14,000	84,000	1	0.125	3,500	19,250	375	23,125
38	Director of Operations	137,000	27,400	164,400	3	0.750	41,100	37,675	1,500	80,275
39	Member of Technical Staff	94,248	18,850	113,098	2	0.375	14,137	25,918	750	40,805
40	Member of Operations Staff	71,000	14,200	85,200	1	0.125	3,550	19,525	375	23,450
41	Director of Marketing	125,000	25,000	150,000	2	0.375	18,750	34,375	750	53,875
42	Member of Technical Staff	65,000	13,000	78,000	1	0.125	3,250	17,875	375	21,500
43	Member of Technical Staff - Nonexempt	42,950	8,590	51,540	1	0.125	2,148	11,811	375	14,334
44	Member of Technical Staff	90,000	18,000	108,000	1	0.125	4,500	24,750	375	29,625
45	Member of Technical Staff	109,000	21,800	130,800	2	0.375	16,350	29,975	750	47,075
46	Member of Operations Staff	84,200	16,840	101,040	1	0.125	4,210	23,155	375	27,740
47	Member of Technical Staff	128,500	25,700	154,200	3	0.750	38,550	35,338	1,500	75,388
48	Member of Technical Staff	80,900	16,180	97,080	1	0.125	4,045	22,248	375	26,668
49	Member of Technical Staff	60,300	12,060	72,360	1	0.125	3,015	16,583	375	19,973
50	Member of Technical Staff	58,500	11,700	70,200	1	0.125	2,925	16,088	375	19,388
51	Director Release and Customer Support	116,000	23,200	139,200	2	0.375	17,400	31,900	750	50,050
52	Executive Assistant	35,000	7,000	42,000	1	0.125	1,750	9,625	375	11,750
53	Member of Technical Staff	113,400	22,680	136,080	2	0.375	17,010	31,185	750	48,945
54	Member of Technical Staff	112,041	22,408	134,449	2	0.375	16,806	30,811	750	48,367
55	Member of Operations Staff	70,000	14,000	84,000	1	0.125	3,500	19,250	375	23,125
56	Member of Technical Staff	77,000	15,400	92,400	2	0.375	11,550	21,175	750	33,475
57	Member of Technical Staff	107,000	21,400	128,400	3	0.750	32,100	29,425	1,500	63,025
58	Director of International Operations	150,000	30,000	180,000	1	0.125	7,500	41,250	375	49,125
59	Member of Technical Staff	110,000	22,000	132,000	2	0.375	16,500	30,250	750	47,500
60	Vice President and General Manager of EMEA	145,000	29,000	174,000	2	0.375	21,750	39,875	750	62,375
61	Account Executive	82,500	16,500	99,000	1	0.125	4,125	22,688	375	27,188
62	Account Executive	75,261	15,052	90,313	2	0.375	11,289	20,697	750	32,736
63	Member of Technical Staff	67,735	13,547	81,282	2	0.375	10,160	18,627	750	29,537
64	Member of Technical Staff	73,350	14,670	88,020	2	0.375	11,003	20,171	750	31,924
65	Member of Technical Staff	99,465	19,893	119,358	3	0.750	29,840	27,353	1,500	58,693

Total 65 $6,134,752 $1,226,950 $7,361,702 $771,073 $1,687,060 $41,625 $2,499,758

Replacement Cost of Assembled Workforce			$2,499,758
Less: Taxes		40.0%	(999,903)
Costs Avoided, Net of Tax			$1,499,855

		Interview & H.R.	
(1) Qualified Replacement Training Months		Hours	Rate
1 = < 3 months		5	$75.00
2 = 3-6 months		10	$75.00
3 = 6-12 months		20	$75.00

Amortization Benefit		
Rate of Return	16.0%	
Tax Rate	40.0%	
Tax Amortization Period	15	
Amortization Benefit		285,967
Fair Value of Assembled Workforce, Rounded		$1,790,000

(2) Source: Karl Malloney, Recruiter

Note: Some amounts may not foot due to rounding.

name X is recognized as representing one of the premier companies in the industry. In most cases, the trade name identifies the top products available in the marketplace. The use of this trade name is considered critical to the continued success of the company and provides for a seamless and invisible ownership change by maintaining continuity in the minds of customers.

> Trade names and trademarks must be considered individually to determine their remaining useful life. Trade names and trademarks that are associated with a company name or logo (e.g., McDonald's) typically have indefinite lives. Many product trade names and trademarks also will have an indefinite life if no reasonable estimate can be made of the end of the product life (e.g., Coca-Cola). However, the analyst must be careful to find out whether there is a planned phaseout of a product or ascertain whether it can be estimated with reasonable certainty that a name will lose value or be abandoned over time. In such a case, a finite life is suggested and therefore an amortization period is warranted. Remember, for tax purposes generally all intangibles are amortizable over a 15-year life.

To value the trade name, the cost approach and the market approach were both considered and then rejected as not being feasible methods of valuation. It is difficult to accurately identify all the costs related to recreating the trade name and building recognition, a factor required to use the cost approach. Trademarks and trade names rarely sell in the marketplace; thus, information required to perform a market approach is rarely available. The most comprehensive method to value the trade name is a variant of the income approach known as the *relief from royalty method*. The premise of this valuation methodology is the assumption that an owner/operator of a company would be compelled to pay the rightful owner of the intangible asset (such as a trade name) if the owner/operator did not have the legal right to utilize the subject intellectual property. Since ownership of a trade name relieves a company from making such payments (royalties), the financial performance of the company is enhanced to the extent that such royalty payments are avoided. The royalty is usually expressed as a percentage of pretax revenues.

The relief from royalty method equates the value of a trademark or trade name to the portion of the company's earnings that represents the pretax royalty that may have been paid for using the trade name. For the name valued, it was determined that a royalty rate of 4 percent is applicable, stated as a percentage of sales.

This pretax royalty rate was selected based on observed royalty rates in the market and on an analysis of the rate that the company's margins could support. Market data was observed in The Financial Valuation Group's proprietary database documenting the range of royalty rates for trademarks to be 1 percent to 10 percent, with the average at 4 percent.

Thus, based largely on a review of publicly available data on trademark/trade name licensing transactions and a comparison of the name recognition between X and the guideline royalties, a 4 percent average royalty rate was selected to value the trade name. The BEV (shown in Exhibit 3.5) indicates that there are ample earnings to allow for this level of royalty payments and still earn a fair return on sales. Target Company could easily pay these royalties if it did not own the right to use the trade name. In management interviews and research, it was determined that the technology was primarily responsible for the company's superior profitability.

The rights to use the trade name transfer to the buyer in perpetuity, giving it an indefinite life. The fair value of the trade name is the present value of the royalties projected for the five-year period of 2002 to 2006, plus the present value of the residual at the end of the five-year period, plus the amortization benefit. A 16 percent rate of return was chosen to reflect a risk assessment that the trade name was approximately as risky as the business overall.

Based on the analysis as presented in Exhibit 3.9, it was concluded that the fair value of the trade name as of the valuation date was $23,760,000 (rounded). This asset has an indefinite life.

Noncompete Agreement

Article X, paragraph 10.1 of the purchase agreement identifies a separate agreement not to compete. The purchase agreement specifies that, for a period of five years commencing at the date of the purchase transaction, the sellers will not engage in any activity that competes with Target Company. One of several accepted methodologies for the valuation of noncompete agreements is to prepare a second BEV analysis, one that assumes that the noncompete agreement is not in place. Presumably, in the absence of such an agreement, the sellers would be free to compete and take business away from Target Company and perhaps cause the company to spend more to defend its position, thus reducing its margins as well. The value of having the noncompete agreement, then, is the difference in the two BEVs, as shown in Exhibit 3.10.

Exhibit 3.9 Target Company—Valuation of Trade Name as of December 31, 2001 ($'000s)

		2002	2003	2004	2005	2006
Net Sales from Business Enterprise Valuation (1)		$69,000	$79,350	$89,269	$98,196	$108,015
Pretax Relief from Royalty	4.0%	$2,760	$3,174	$3,571	$3,928	$4,321
Income Tax Liability	40.0%	1,104	1,270	1,428	1,571	1,728
After-Tax Royalty		1,656	1,904	2,142	2,357	2,592
Present Value Income Factor	16.0%	0.9285	0.8004	0.6900	0.5948	0.5128
Present Value Relief from Royalty		$1,538	$1,524	$1,478	$1,402	$1,329
Sum of Present Value Relief from Royalty, 2002—2006		$7,271				
Residual Calculation:						
2006 After-Tax Royalty		$2,592				
2007 After-Tax Royalty, Assuming Growth of	5.0%	$2,722				
Residual Capitalization Rate		11.0%				
Residual Value, 2007		$24,742				
Present Value Factor		0.5128				
Fair Market Value of Residual			12,687			
Present Value of Trade Name Royalty Flows			$19,959			
Amortization Benefit						
Discount Rate	16.0%					
Tax Rate	40.0%					
Tax Amortization Period	15					
Amortization Benefit			3,805			
Fair Value of Trade Name, Rounded			$23,760			
(1) Figures shown from Business Enterprise Valuation (Exhibit 3.5)						

Note: Some amounts may not foot due to rounding.

In the interest of brevity and because a full BEV analysis has been presented as an example, explanations of the assumptions will not be repeated, except those assumptions that change. Under the assumption of competition, sellers could negatively impact Target Company, affecting the growth of sales (i.e., the seller, if not under a noncompete agreement could theoretically go to work for a competitor or start a new company and cause Target Company to grow more slowly than otherwise projected) and cause it to incur more marketing and other expenses. Thus, the changed assumptions are:

	BEV **Without Competition** **Exhibit 3.5**	**BEV** **With Competition** **Exhibit 3.10**
Net sales growth rate		
Year one	15%	10%
Year two	15%	10%
Operating expenses		
Year one	30%	32%
Year two	29%	30%

Exhibit 3.10 Target Company—Valuation of Noncompete as of December 31, 2001 ($'000s)

		FORECAST			
CASH FLOWS (WITHOUT NONCOMPETE IN PLACE)	**ACTUAL 2001**	**2002**	**2003**	**2004**	**2005**
Sales Growth Percentage (1)		10.0%	10.0%	12.5%	10.0%
Net Sales	$60,000	$66,000	$72,600	$81,675	$89,843
Cost of Sales Percentage (1)	40.0%	40.0%	39.0%	39.0%	39.0%
Cost of Sales	$24,000	$26,400	$28,314	$31,853	$35,039
Gross Profit	36,000	39,600	44,286	49,822	54,804
Operating Expense Percentage (1)	30.0%	32.0%	30.0%	29.0%	29.0%
Operating Expenses	$18,000	$21,120	$21,780	$23,686	$26,054
Depreciation (MACRS)	1,750	3,097	5,171	3,961	3,120
Amortization of Intangibles (Tax)	0	8,433	8,433	8,433	8,433
Total Operating Expenses	19,750	32,650	35,384	36,080	37,607
Taxable Income	16,250	6,950	8,902	13,741	17,197
Income Taxes	6,500	2,780	3,561	5,497	6,879
Net Income	$9,750	$4,170	$5,341	$8,245	$10,318
Net Cash Flow					
Net Income		$4,170	$5,341	$8,245	$10,318
Capital Expenditures		(660)	(726)	(817)	(898)
Change in Working Capital		6,600	(990)	(1,361)	(1,225)
Depreciation		3,097	5,171	3,961	3,120
Amortization of Intangibles (Tax)		8,433	8,433	8,433	8,433
Net Cash Flow		21,640	17,229	18,461	19,747
Present Value Factor, where Discount Rate =	16.0%	0.9285	0.8004	0.6900	0.5948
Present Value of Net Cash Flow		$20,092	$13,790	$12,739	$11,746
2011 Cash Flow		$28,331			
Less: Tax Benefit of Amortization		(3,373)			
2011 Cash Flow, net of Benefit		$24,958			
2012 Cash Flow, Assuming Growth of	5.0%	$26,205			
Residual Capitalization Rate		11.00%			
Residual Value, 2012		$238,231			
Present Value Factor		0.2441			
Fair Value of Residual		$58,163			
Net Present Value of Net Cash Flow, **2002-2011**		$111,055			
Net Present Value of Residual Cash Flow		58,163			
Present Value of Amortization Tax Benefit, 2012-2016		2,697			
Total Invested Capital **with Competition,** Rounded		$172,000			
Business Enterprise Value (Exhibit 3.5)		185,000			
Difference = Gross Value of Noncompete		$13,000			
Times: Probability Factor (2)		60.0%			
Probability Adjusted Value of Noncompete		$7,800			
Amortization Benefit					
Discount Rate	16.0%				
Tax Rate	40.0%				
Tax Amortization Period	15				
Amortization Benefit		1,486			
Fair Value of Noncompete Agreement, Rounded		$9,300			

(1) Percentages based on assumption of competition. See discussion in **Noncompete** Section of Chapter 3.
(2) To account for likelihood of competing absent an agreement and likelihood of success.

Note: Some amounts may not foot due to rounding.

	FORECAST					
	2006	2007	2008	2009	2010	2011
	10.0%	7.5%	7.5%	7.5%	7.5%	7.5%
	$98,827	$106,239	$114,207	$122,772	$131,980	$141,879
	39.0%	39.0%	39.0%	39.0%	39.0%	39.0%
	$38,542	$41,433	$44,541	$47,881	$51,472	$55,333
	60,284	64,806	69,666	74,891	80,508	86,546
	29.0%	29.0%	29.0%	29.0%	29.0%	29.0%
	$28,660	$30,809	$33,120	$35,604	$38,274	$41,145
	2,544	2,649	2,762	2,011	1,246	1,551
	8,433	8,433	8,433	8,433	8,433	8,433
	39,637	41,891	44,315	46,048	47,953	51,129
	20,647	22,915	25,351	28,843	32,555	35,417
	8,259	9,166	10,140	11,537	13,022	14,167
	$12,388	$13,749	$15,210	$17,306	$19,533	$21,250
	$12,388	$13,749	$15,210	$17,306	$19,533	$21,250
	(988)	(1,062)	(1,142)	(1,228)	(1,320)	(1,419)
	(1,348)	(1,112)	(1,195)	(1,285)	(1,381)	(1,485)
	2,544	2,649	2,762	2,011	1,246	1,551
	8,433	8,433	8,433	8,433	8,433	8,433
	21,030	22,656	24,069	25,237	26,511	28,331
	0.5128	0.4421	0.3811	0.3285	0.2832	0.2441
	$10,784	$10,015	$9,172	$8,291	$7,508	$6,917

	2012	2013	2014	2015	2016
Amortization of Intangibles (Pretax)	$8,433	$8,433	$8,433	$8,433	$8,433
Tax Benefit of Amortization	3,373	3,373	3,373	3,373	3,373
Present Value Factor	0.2105	0.1814	0.1564	0.1348	0.1162
Present Value of Tax Benefit	$710	$612	$528	$455	$392
Sum = Fair Value of Tax Benefit	$2,697				

The resulting BEV (with competition) is $172,000,000 (rounded). The value of the noncompete agreement under these assumptions is:

	Invested Capital
BEV with agreement in place (rounded)	$185,000,000
BEV without agreement in place (rounded)	172,000,000
Difference equals gross value of agreement	$ 13,000,000

The gross value of the noncompete agreement calculated above represents the difference in value of the BEV without competition and the BEV with competition. Implicit in the analysis to this point is that, absent a noncompete agreement, the sellers would compete immediately with Target Company, either by joining a competitor or starting a new company, and would be successful in their effort. In fact, there is at least some probability that the sellers would not compete and a probability that even if they did, they would not be successful. Thus, the gross value of the agreement is reduced to account for these probabilities. The probability factor is somewhat judgmental and is developed by discussing the issue with the individuals under the noncompete, as well as company management. After due consideration of these issues, the probability factor was estimated to be 60 percent.

The gross value of the noncompete agreement is multiplied by the 60 percent probability factor. The result is the probability-adjusted value of the noncompete agreement, $7,800,000. After adding the amortization benefit, the fair value of the noncompete agreement is $9,300,000 (rounded). The remaining useful life is five years.

Technology

The value of the company's developed technology was determined using a form of the income approach known as the multi-period excess earnings method. This method measures the present value of the future earnings to be generated during the remaining lives of the assets. Using the BEV as a starting point, pretax cash flows attributable to the technology that existed at the valuation date were calculated. This was accomplished by utilizing management's forecast of sales attributable to the existing technology. These sales were estimated at 2001 levels plus a growth rate commensurate with inflation, or 3 percent per year. As with the BEV, deductions are made for cost of goods sold (40 percent of sales attributable to existing technology in 2002, and 39 percent after 2002) and operating expenses (20 percent of sales in 2002, then 19 percent, after deducting estimated development expenses of 10 percent from the operating expense base to reflect the fact that the developed technology should not be burdened by expenses of developing new technology). Contributory charges on the other identified assets were taken.

Returns on and of or *contributory charges* represent charges for the use of contributory assets employed to support the technology-based assets and help generate revenue. The cash flows from the technology-based assets must support charges for replacement of assets employed and provide a fair return to the owners of capital. The respective rates of return, while subjective, are directly related to the analyst's assessment of the risk inherent in each asset.

The following table from the IPR&D Practice Aid provides examples of assets typically treated as contributory assets, and suggested bases for determining the fair return. Generally, it is presumed that the *return of* the asset is reflected in the operating costs when applicable (for example, depreciation expense). The contributory asset charge is "the product of the asset's fair value and the required rate of return on the asset."[14]

Asset	Basis of Charge
Working capital	Short-term lending rates for market participants (e.g., working capital lines or short-term revolver rates)
Fixed assets (e.g., property, plant, and equipment)	Financing rate for similar assets for market participants (e.g., terms offered by vendor financing), or rates implied by operating leases, capital leases, or both, typically segregated between returns of (i.e., recapture of investment) and returns on.
Workforce (which is not recognized separately from goodwill), customer lists, trademarks, and trade names	Weighted average cost of capital (WACC) for young, single-product companies (may be lower than discount rate applicable to a particular project).

Patents	WACC for young, single-product companies (may be lower than discount rate applicable to a particular project). In cases where risk of realizing economic value of patent is close to or the same as risk of realizing a project, rates would be equivalent to that of the project.
Other intangibles, including base (or core) technology	Rates appropriate to the risk of the subject intangible. When market evidence is available, it should be used. In other cases, rates should be consistent with the relative risk of other assets in the analysis and should be higher for riskier assets.[15]

It is important to note that the assumed fair value of the contributory asset is not necessarily static over time. Working capital and tangible assets may fluctuate throughout the forecast period, and returns are typically taken on estimated average balances in each year. Average balances of tangible assets subject to accelerated depreciation (as is the case here) may decline as the depreciation outstrips capital expenditures in the early years of the forecast. While the carrying value of amortizable intangible assets declines over time, there is a presumption that such assets are replenished each year, so the contributory charge usually takes the form of a fixed charge each year. An exception to this rule is a noncompete agreement, which is not replenished and does not function as a supporting asset past its expiration period.

The return requirements used here are after-tax and are:

Contributory Asset Charges

Working capital	5.0%
Land and building	7.0%
Machinery and equipment	8.0%
Software	18.0%
Trade name	16.0%
Noncompete agreement	16.0%
Assembled workforce	16.0%
Customer base	18.0%

Those guidelines are generally followed here, although it should be noted that some practitioners use a specific "mini-WACC" for fixed assets (the weights reflecting the percentage financed [debt] and the percentage down [equity]). Lease rates are also sometimes used.

Required returns were deducted from the cash flows. *Returns on* working capital and fixed assets are taken on the average book balances for each year in the projection period, as determined in the development of the BEV. The *return of* is satisfied through the replenishment of the asset through ongoing expenditures. Contributory charges on the intangible assets are taken on the fair value at acquisition. The returns of these assets are satisfied by that portion of operating expenses that relate to the replenishment of the various intangibles. Total returns are allocated among the intangibles valued using the multiperiod excess earnings method (here, developed technology and in-process research and development), usually on the basis of relative revenues, as presented in Exhibit 3.11.

We then performed a study related to the expected life of the technology, which produced a four-year remaining useful life, during which the asset is projected to function at 100 percent (i.e., no economic deterioration) in 2002, 90 percent in 2003, 80 percent in 2004, and 50 percent productivity in year four. Such a study may be performed in several different ways, depending on the intangible.[16] Here, the "survivor curve" was developed through detailed discussions with technical and marketing managers. It should be noted that some practitioners prefer to account for declining productivity of the asset by use of a declining revenue curve. The surviving cash flows (the excess cash flows multiplied by the projected survivorship of the technology in each year), after providing for returns on the other assets, are attributable to the technology. The discount rate of 18 percent reflects the higher relative risk of this asset compared with the business overall and the other intangibles.

Based on our analysis, we concluded that the fair value of the acquired technology on the valuation date was $13,500,000 (rounded), as shown in Exhibit 3.12. As with the other intangible assets, the value is determined after deducting an income tax charge and adding an amortization benefit. The asset's remaining useful life is four years, but the survivor curve provides a means to record future amortization consistent with the contribution to cash flows in each year, rather than by the straight-line method.

In-Process Research and Development

The value of the in-process research and development was also estimated using the multiperiod excess earnings method. Similar to the methodology for valuing the technology, the discounted cash flow

Exhibit 3.11   Target Company—Valuation of Technology as of December 31, 2001 ($'000s)

CALCULATION OF CONTRIBUTORY ASSET CHARGES

Contributory Asset

A. Asset Balances		2002	2003	2004	2005	2006
Net Working Capital		$13,425	$11,126	$12,646	$14,060	$15,466
Land and Buildings		21,934	21,815	21,718	21,640	21,580
Machinery and Equipment, net		17,849	14,551	10,900	8,348	6,582
Software		7,070	7,070	7,070	7,070	7,070
Trade Name		23,760	23,760	23,760	23,760	23,760
Noncompete Agreement		9,300	9,300	9,300	9,300	9,300
Assembled Workforce		1,790	1,790	1,790	1,790	1,790
Customer Base		6,490	6,490	6,490	6,490	6,490

B. Total Returns	Rate	2002	2003	2004	2005	2006
Net Working Capital	5.0%	$671	$556	$632	$703	$773
Land and Buildings	7.0%	1,535	1,527	1,520	1,515	1,511
Machinery and Equipment, net	8.0%	1,428	1,164	872	668	527
Software	18.0%	1,273	1,273	1,273	1,273	1,273
Trade Name	16.0%	3,802	3,802	3,802	3,802	3,802
Noncompete Agreement	16.0%	1,488	1,488	1,488	1,488	1,488
Assembled Workforce	16.0%	286	286	286	286	286
Customer Base	18.0%	1,168	1,168	1,168	1,168	1,168

C. Distribution of Revenues	2002	2003	2004	2005	2006
Technology	$61,800	$63,654	$65,564	$67,531	$69,556
IPR&D	7,200	15,696	23,705	30,665	38,459
Total DCF Revenues	$69,000	$79,350	$89,269	$98,196	$108,015
Technology Percent	89.57%	80.22%	73.45%	68.77%	64.40%
IPR&D Percent	10.43%	19.78%	26.55%	31.23%	35.60%
Total	100.00%	100.00%	100.00%	100.00%	100.00%

D. Allocated Returns—Technology	2002	2003	2004	2005	
Net Working Capital	$601	$446	$464	$483	
Land and Buildings	1,375	1,225	1,117	1,042	
Machinery and Equipment, net	1,279	934	640	459	
Software	1,140	1,021	935	875	
Trade Name	3,405	3,050	2,792	2,614	
Noncompete Agreement	1,333	1,194	1,093	1,023	
Assembled Workforce	257	230	210	197	
Customer Base	1,046	937	858	803	
Total	$10,436	$9,036	$8,109	$7,498	

E. Allocated Returns—IPR&D	2002	2003	2004	2005	2006
Net Working Capital	$70	$110	$168	$220	$275
Land and Buildings	160	302	404	473	538
Machinery and Equipment, net	149	230	232	209	187
Software	133	252	338	397	453
Trade Name	397	752	1,010	1,187	1,354
Noncompete Agreement	155	294	395	465	530
Assembled Workforce	30	57	76	89	102
Customer Base	122	231	310	365	416
Total	$1,216	$2,228	$2,932	$3,405	$3,855

Note: Some amounts may not foot due to rounding.

model was constructed starting with expected sales based on the technology that was in process at the valuation date. For simplicity, it is assumed that the IPR&D will be completed in early 2002 and is projected to produce sales of $7,200,000. Sales are further projected to increase rapidly in subsequent years. Similar to the technology valuation, cost of sales (40 percent of sales in 2002, 39 percent thereafter) and operating expenses (20 percent of sales [excluding any synergies] in 2002, 19 percent thereafter, and net of development costs, which will no longer occur relative to this technology) are forecast, as is the cost to complete

Exhibit 3.12   Target Company—Valuation of Technology as of December 31, 2001 ($'000s)

	ACTUAL	FORECAST			
	2001	2002	2003	2004	2005
Net Sales—ExistingTechnology (1)	$60,000	$61,800	$63,654	$65,564	$67,531
Cost of Sales	24,000	24,720	24,825	25,570	26,337
Gross Profit	36,000	37,080	38,829	39,994	41,194
Operating Expenses (2)	12,000	12,360	12,094	12,457	12,831
Depreciation	1,750	2,774	4,148	2,909	2,145
Total Operating Expenses	13,750	15,134	16,242	15,366	14,976
Taxable Income	22,250	21,946	22,587	24,627	26,217
Income Taxes	8,900	8,778	9,035	9,851	10,487
Net Income	$13,350	$13,168	$13,552	$14,776	$15,730

Residual Cash Flow Attributable to Technology

Less Returns on						
16,500	Net Working Capital	5.0%	$601	$446	$464	$483
22,000	Land and Buildings	7.0%	1,375	1,225	1,117	1,042
19,000	Machinery and Equipment, net	8.0%	1,279	934	640	459
7,070	Software	18.0%	1,140	1,021	935	875
23,760	Trade Name	16.0%	3,405	3,050	2,792	2,614
9,300	Noncompete Agreement	16.0%	1,333	1,194	1,093	1,023
1,790	Assembled Workforce	16.0%	257	230	210	197
6,490	Customer Base	18.0%	1,046	937	858	803
	Sum of Returns		$10,436	$9,036	$8,109	$7,498
	After-Tax Residual Cash Flows		$2,732	$4,516	$6,667	$8,233
	Survivorship of Technology (3)		100.0%	90.0%	80.0%	50.0%
	Surviving Residual Cash Flows		$2,732	$4,064	$5,334	$4,116
18.00%	Present Value Factor for Residual Cash Flow		0.9206	0.7801	0.6611	0.5603
	Present Value of Surviving Residual Cash Flows		$2,515	$3,171	$3,526	$2,306

Sum of Present Values, 2002–2005		$11,519		
Amortization Benefit				
Discount Rate	18.0%			
Tax Rate	40.0%			
Tax Amortization Period	15			
Amortization Benefit		1,993		
Fair Value of Technology, Rounded		$13,500		

(1) Based on 2001 actual sales, with growth attritubutable to existing technology.
(2) Excludes development expenses of 10 percent to reflect that developed technology
  should not be burdened by the expenses of developing new technology.
(3) Assumes 4 year life.

Note: Some amounts may not foot due to rounding.

the project. The useful life of the IPR&D was estimated to be five years, during which the technology is projected to function at 100 percent for the first year, then decline in productivity to 85 percent in 2003, 75 percent in 2004, 60 percent in 2005, and 50 percent in 2006. In addition, estimated required returns *on* and *of* the assets (see previous section) were taken.

It is assumed for purposes of this example that the IPR&D is a brand-new, stand-alone technology not supported by the base or core technology, defined as technology that has value through its use or continued reuse within a product family.[17] If an IPR&D project is supported by a core or base technology, a contributory charge must be assessed.

The sum of the present values is $3,833,000. A discount rate of 25 percent was selected to reflect the additional risk of the unproven technology.[18] After accounting for the amortization benefit, it was concluded that the fair value of the IPR&D as of December 31, 2001, was $4,330,000 (Exhibit 3.13). This asset's estimated remaining useful life is five years, but, as with existing technology, the survivor curve provides a means to record future amortization consistent with the contribution to cash flows in each year.

Valuation of Goodwill

In the valuation of a successful business enterprise, there are often intangible assets that cannot be separately identified. These intangible assets are generally referred to as goodwill. The term *goodwill*, however, is sometimes used to describe the aggregate of all of the intangible assets of a business. In a more restricted sense, goodwill is the sum total of only the imponderable qualities that attract future new customers to the business.

In the final analysis, goodwill equates with the residual intangible asset that generates earnings in excess of a normal return on all the other tangible and intangible assets. The present value of future cash flows contributing to goodwill at the time of acquisition can be calculated by summing the future excess earnings, then discounting to present value. Assuming all of the tangible and intangible assets have been identified and valued at the acquisition date, this process is simplified by use of the residual method. Under the residual method, the present value of the future excess earnings, or goodwill, is calculated by subtracting from the adjusted purchase price the fair value of all the identified tangible and intangible assets. The remainder or residual amount equates with goodwill. Keep in mind that under GAAP goodwill includes assembled workforce, but assembled workforce was separately valued to obtain a contributory return for IPR&D and technology. As a result and pursuant to SFAS No. 141, the indicated value of assembled workforce must be added to the indicated value of goodwill to arrive at the fair value of goodwill for financial statement reporting purposes.[19]

For financial reporting purposes, included in the goodwill value is the fair value of the assembled workforce of $1,790,000. Based on this

Exhibit 3.13 Target Company—Valuation of In-Process Research and Development as of December 31, 2001 ($'000s)

		FORECAST				
		2002	2003	2004	2005	2006
Net Sales—New Technology (1)		$7,200	$15,696	$23,705	$30,665	$38,459
Cost of Sales		2,880	6,121	9,245	11,959	14,999
Gross Profit		4,320	9,575	14,460	18,706	23,460
Operating Expenses (2)		1,440	2,982	4,504	5,826	7,307
Cost to Complete		300	0	0	0	0
Depreciation		323	1,023	1,052	974	906
Total Operating Expenses		2,063	4,005	5,556	6,801	8,213
Taxable Income		2,257	5,570	8,904	11,905	15,247
Income Taxes		903	2,228	3,562	4,762	6,099
Net Income		$1,354	$3,342	$5,343	$7,143	$9,148
Residual Cash Flow Attributable to Technology						
Less Returns on						
$16,500 Net Working Capital	5.0%	$70	$110	$168	$220	$275
22,000 Land and Buildings	7.0%	160	302	404	473	538
19,000 Machinery and Equipment, net	8.0%	149	230	232	209	187
7,070 Software	18.0%	133	252	338	397	453
23,760 Trade Name	16.0%	397	752	1,010	1,187	1,354
9,300 Noncompete Agreement	16.0%	155	294	395	465	530
1,790 Assembled Workforce	16.0%	30	57	76	89	102
6,490 Customer Base	18.0%	122	231	310	365	416
Sum of Returns		$1,216	$2,228	$2,932	$3,405	$3,855
After-Tax Residual Cash Flows		$138	$1,114	$2,411	$3,738	$5,293
Survivorship of Technology (3)		100.0%	85.0%	75.0%	60.0%	50.0%
Surviving Excess Cash Flows		$138	$947	$1,808	$2,243	$2,647
25.0% Present Value Factor for Residual Cash Flow		0.8944	0.7155	0.5724	0.4579	0.3664
Present Value of Surviving Residual Cash Flows		$124	$677	$1,035	$1,027	$970
Sum of Present Values, 2002–2006		$3,833				
Amortization Benefit						
Discount Rate	25.0%					
Tax Rate	40.0%					
Tax Amortization Period	15					
Amortization Benefit		498				
Fair Value of IPR&D Rounded		$4,330				

(1) Based on Business Enterprise Value (Exhibit 3.5), less sales due to existing Technology (Exhibit 3.12).
(2) Excludes development expenses of 10 percent to reflect no future development costs relative to this technology.
(3) Assumes 5 year life.

Note: Some amounts may not foot due to rounding

analysis, the fair value of residual goodwill on December 31, 2001, was $62,050,000 (see Exhibit 3.14).

Allocation of Purchase Price

The summary allocation of values is presented in Exhibit 3.15. In this exhibit, the valuation conclusions are separated into three groups: total current and tangible assets, total intangible assets, and goodwill. Individual asset valuations are presented within each group.

In addition to presenting the summary of values, this schedule pro-

Exhibit 3.14   Target Company—Valuation of Goodwill as of December 31, 2001 ($'000s)

Cash and Acquisition Costs	$150,000
Debt-Free Current Liabilities	25,000
Current Maturities of Long-Term Debt	4,000
Long-Term Debt	30,000
Adjusted Purchase Price	209,000
Less: Fair Value of Current Assets	(41,500)
Less: Fair Value of Tangible Assets	(41,000)
Less: Fair Value of Intangible Assets	
Software	(7,070)
Customer Base	(6,490)
Trade Name	(23,760)
Noncompete Agreement	(9,300)
Technology	(13,500)
In-Process Research and Development	(4,330)
Residual Goodwill	$62,050

Note: Some amounts may not foot due to rounding.

vides a sanity check in the form of a weighted return calculation. The weighted return calculation employs the rate of return for each asset weighted according to its fair value relative to the whole. The weighted return should approximate the overall weighted average cost of capital for the business, although the rates may not exactly be equal because the WACC equates to the business's invested capital (here, $184,000,000) while the weighted return calculation represents total asset value ($209,000,000).

The returns for each asset are those actually used in the foregoing valuation methodology; that is, for tangible assets and contributory intangible assets. For contributory intangible assets that were valued using a form of the income approach (trade name and noncompete agreement), the return is equal to the discount rate used to value that asset. Finally, the return for the assets valued under the excess earnings approach is also their discount rate.

It should be clear that the one asset that does not have a return is goodwill and, admittedly, the return assigned is determined by trial

Exhibit 3.15   Target Company—Valuation Summary as of December 31, 2001 ($'000s)

ASSET NAME	FAIR MARKET VALUE	RETURN	PERCENT TO PURCHASE PRICE	WEIGHTED RETURN
Cash	$1,500	5.00%	0.7%	0.04%
Investments in Marketable Securities	8,000	5.00%	3.8%	0.19%
Accounts Receivable	17,000	5.00%	8.1%	0.41%
Inventory	12,000	5.00%	5.7%	0.29%
Prepaid Expenses	3,000	5.00%	1.4%	0.07%
Land and Buildings	22,000	7.00%	10.5%	0.74%
Machinery and Equipment, net	19,000	8.00%	9.1%	0.73%
TOTAL CURRENT AND TANGIBLE ASSETS	$82,500			
Software	$7,070	18.00%	3.4%	0.61%
Technology	13,500	18.00%	6.5%	1.16%
In-Process Research and Development	4,330	25.00%	2.1%	0.52%
Trade Name	23,760	16.00%	11.4%	1.82%
Customer Base	6,490	18.00%	3.1%	0.56%
Assembled Workforce	1,790	16.00%	0.9%	0.14%
Noncompete Agreement	9,300	16.00%	4.4%	0.71%
TOTAL INTANGIBLE ASSETS	$66,240			
GOODWILL (excluding assembled workforce)	$60,260	28.00%	28.8%	8.07%
TOTAL ASSETS	$209,000			16.05%

Note: For financial reporting purposes, the fair value of goodwill includes the fair value of assembled workforce for a total fair value of residual goodwill of $62,050,000.

Note: Some amounts may not foot due to rounding.

and error. The goodwill return is imputed based on the overall weighted return needed to equal the weighted average cost of capital. By its nature, goodwill is the riskiest asset of the group and therefore should require a higher return than the overall business return. If a goodwill return of, say, 10 percent is required to achieve a weighted return of approximately 16 percent, this signals a problem, and the analyst will have to go back and review and revise the work—something is wrong! In this calculation, the goodwill return of 28 percent suggests that goodwill is riskier than all of the other assets but, at a return of 28 percent, still well within reason for a proven going concern. Thus, the returns chosen for each asset are reasonable.

Chapter 4

SFAS No. 142, Impairment of Goodwill and Other Intangible Assets

SFAS No. 142 applies to all acquired intangible assets, whether acquired singly, as part of a group, or in a business combination. The Statement mandates that goodwill and intangible assets without a defined life shall not be amortized over a defined period; rather, they must be tested for impairment at least annually at the "reporting unit" level. Although the Financial Accounting Standards Board (FASB) already had addressed asset impairment (originally SFAS No. 121, *Accounting for the Impairment of Long-Lived Assets and for Long-Lived Assets to Be Disposed Of*, now superceded by SFAS No. 144, *Accounting for the Impairment or Disposal of Long-Lived Assets*), goodwill and intangible assets with an indefinite life must be tested for impairment exclusively under the guidelines of SFAS No. 142.[1]

All goodwill reported in the financial statements of a reporting unit should be tested for impairment as if the reporting unit were a stand-alone entity. A *reporting unit* is an operating segment (see SFAS No. 131, *Disclosures About Segments of an Enterprise and Related Information*) or one level below an operating segment (called a component). A component of an operating segment is a reporting unit if the component constitutes a business for which discrete financial information is available and segment management regularly reviews the operating results of that component. Goodwill must be defined and allocated at this component level. Entities that are not required to report segment information in accordance with SFAS No. 131 are nevertheless required to test goodwill for impairment at the reporting unit level.[2]

The nature of fair value of a reporting unit is that the synergies of operating in a combined entity, especially for shared overhead costs, are a fundamental part of the fair value of a reporting unit. SFAS No. 142 states:

> Substantial value may arise from the ability to take advantage of synergies and other benefits that flow from control over another entity. Consequently, measuring the fair value of a collection of assets and liabilities that operate together in a controlled entity is different from measuring the fair value of that entity's individual equity securities.[3]

Additionally, if you could not take into account the synergies of being part of a combined entity, there would be an immediate impairment, since such economy of scale synergies are a typical part of a control transaction.

All acquired goodwill should be assigned to reporting units. This will critically depend on the assignment of other acquired assets and assumed liabilities. These assets and liabilities will be assigned to reporting units based on the following criteria:

- The asset will be employed in or the liability relates to the operations of a reporting unit
- The asset or liability will be considered in determining the fair value of the reporting unit[4]

Goodwill is the excess of cost over the assets acquired and liabilities assumed, but this definition is deceptively simple. The amount of goodwill allocated to a reporting unit is contingent upon the expected benefits from the synergies of the combination.[5] This goodwill allocation is required even though other assets or liabilities of the acquired entity may not be assigned to that reporting unit, that is, they may be assigned to other reporting units. A relative fair value allocation approach similar to that used when a portion of a reporting unit is disposed of (see SFAS No. 144) should be used to determine how goodwill should be allocated when an entity reorganizes its reporting structure in a manner that changes the composition of one or more of its reporting units. Otherwise, SFAS No. 144 should not be followed. Rather, goodwill should be tested for impairment pursuant to SFAS No. 142.[6]

The measurement of the fair value of intangibles and goodwill can be performed at any time during the fiscal year as long as the timing is consistent from year to year. Although different measurement dates can be used for different reporting units, whichever date is selected for a reporting unit must be consistent from year to year. A detailed determination of the fair value of a reporting unit may be carried forward from one year to the next (i.e., no further impairment analysis is required) if *all* of the following criteria are met:

- The assets and liabilities that comprise the reporting unit have not changed significantly since the most recent fair value determination.
- The most recent fair value determination results in an amount that exceeds the carrying amount of the reporting unit by a substantial margin.
- Based on an analysis of events, it is determined that the possibility is remote that a fair value determination will be less than the current carrying amount of the reporting unit.[7]

However, the annual impairment test is to be accelerated and goodwill of a reporting unit should be tested for impairment on an interim basis if an event occurs that would more likely than not reduce the fair value of a reporting unit below its carrying value. Examples of such events are:

- A significant adverse change in legal factors or in the business climate
- An adverse action or assessment by a regulator
- Unanticipated competition
- A loss of key personnel
- A more-likely-than-not expectation that a reporting unit or a significant portion of a reporting unit will be sold or otherwise disposed of
- The testing for recoverability under SFAS No. 144 of a significant asset group within a reporting unit
- Recognition of a goodwill impairment loss in the financial statements of a subsidiary that is a component of a reporting unit[8]

NATURE OF GOODWILL

The definition of goodwill warrants repeating: Goodwill is the excess of the cost of an acquired entity over the net of amounts assigned to assets acquired and liabilities assumed.[9] For GAAP purposes, goodwill includes all amounts that fail the criteria of an identified intangible asset. Importantly, the practitioner must understand that the nature of goodwill for financial reporting is different from that used in a legal setting. Such "legal goodwill" is generally considered to be all value above tangible asset value. For financial reporting, it helps to consider the elements of goodwill as:

- The excess of the fair values over the book values of the acquired entity's net assets at the date of acquisition.
- The fair values of other net assets that had not been recognized by the acquired entity at the date of acquisition.
- The fair value of the *going-concern* element of the acquired entity's existing business. The going-concern element represents the ability of the established business to earn a higher rate of return on an assembled collection of net assets than would be expected if those net assets had to be acquired separately.
- The fair value of the expected synergies and other benefits from combining the acquiring entity's and acquired entity's net assets and businesses; those synergies and other benefits are unique to each combination, and different combinations would produce different synergies and, hence, different values.
- Overvaluation of the consideration paid by the acquiring entity stemming from errors in valuing the consideration tendered.
- Overpayment or underpayment by the acquiring entity. Overpayment might occur, for example, if the price is driven up in the course of bidding for the acquired entity, while underpayment may occur in the case of a distress sale or fire sale.[10]

The FASB explained its rationale for including the above elements this way:

- The Board continues to believe that the following analysis of those components is useful in understanding the nature of goodwill. The first two components, both of which relate to the acquired entity, conceptually are not part of goodwill. The first component is not an asset in and of itself but instead reflects gains that were not recognized by the acquired entity on its net assets. As such, that component is part of those assets rather than part of goodwill. The second component also is not part of goodwill conceptually; it primarily reflects intangible assets that might be recognized as individual assets.

- As the Board noted in both the 1999 Exposure Draft and the 2001 Exposure Draft, the third and fourth components *are* conceptually part of goodwill. The third component relates to the acquired entity and reflects the excess assembled value of the acquired entity's net assets. It represents the preexisting goodwill that was either internally generated by the acquired entity or acquired by it in prior business combinations. The fourth component relates to the acquired entity and acquiring entity jointly and reflects the excess assembled value that is created by the combination—the synergies that are expected from combining those businesses. The Board described the third and fourth components collectively as "core goodwill."

- The fifth and sixth components, both of which relate to the acquiring entity, also are not conceptually part of goodwill. The fifth component is not an asset in and of itself or even part of an asset but, rather, is a measurement error. The sixth component also is not an asset; conceptually it represents a loss (in the case of overpayment) or a gain (in the case of underpayment) to the acquiring entity. Thus, neither of those components is conceptually part of goodwill.[11]

GOODWILL, INDEFINITE-LIVED INTANGIBLE ASSETS, AND THE IMPAIRMENT TEST

A recognized intangible asset shall be amortized over its useful life to the reporting entity unless that life is determined to be indefinite.[12] If no legal, regulatory, contractual, competitive, economic, or other factors limit the useful life of the asset of an intangible asset to the reporting entity, the useful life of the asset shall be considered to be indefinite. The term *indefinite* does not mean infinite.[13] An intangible asset that is not subject to amortization (an indefinite life intangible) shall be tested for impairment in the same manner as goodwill. Such intangibles are tested annually or upon triggering events.[14]

Under SFAS No. 142, amortization of goodwill and indefinite-lived intangible assets is not allowed—such goodwill and intangible assets are tested annually for impairment. The impairment test is a two-step process. First, the fair value of the reporting unit is determined and compared with the carrying value of the reporting unit, including goodwill.

The fair value of a reporting unit refers to the amount at which the unit as a whole could be bought or sold in a current transaction between willing parties. Quoted market prices in active markets are considered the best evidence of fair value and should be used as the basis for the measurement, if available. However, the market price of an individual share of stock (and thus the market capitalization of a reporting unit with publicly traded stock) may not be representative of the fair value of the reporting unit as a whole. Certainly, stock prices rise and fall over time and a stock price that is comparatively low at a certain date may not be indicative of impairment, which has a connotation of permanence. Therefore, the quoted market price of an individual share of stock need not be the sole measurement basis of the fair value of a reporting unit. If a quoted market price of the shares of a reporting unit is not available, the estimate of fair value should be based on the best information available, including prices for similar assets and liabilities and the results of other valuation techniques. A valuation technique based on multiples of earnings, revenue, or a similar performance measure may be used to estimate the fair value of a reporting unit if that technique is consistent with the objective of measuring fair value. Such measures may be appropriate, for example, when the fair value of an entity that has comparable operations and economic characteristics is observable and the relevant multiples of a comparable entity are known. Conversely, use of multiples would not be appropriate in situations in which the operations or activities of an entity for which the multiples are known are not of a comparable nature, scope, or size as the reporting unit for which fair value is being estimated.[15]

SFAS No. 142 states:

A present value technique is often the best available technique with which to estimate the fair value of a group of net assets (such as a reporting unit). If a present value technique is used to measure fair value, estimates of future cash flows . . . shall be consistent with the objective of measuring fair value. Those cash flow estimates shall incorporate assumptions that marketplace participants would use in their estimates of fair value. If that information is not available without undue cost and effort, an entity may use its own assumptions. Those cash flow estimates shall be based on reasonable and supportable assumptions and shall consider all available evidence. The weight given to the evidence shall be commensurate with the extent to which the evidence can be verified objectively. If a range is estimated for the amounts or timing of possible cash flows, the likelihood of possible outcomes shall be considered. [see FASB Statement of Financial Concepts 7 [Conc. 7], *Using Cash Flow Information and Present Value in Accounting Measurements*].[16]

Goodwill impairment exists if the carrying value of the reporting unit, including goodwill, exceeds the fair value of the reporting unit. In such a case, the second step of the goodwill impairment test is triggered.

The second step of the goodwill impairment test requires performing what amounts to a new purchase price allocation as of the date of the impairment test—as if a business combination were consummated on the date of the impairment test. The new valuation work should include determining the new fair values of both the originally recognized assets and any new assets that may have been unrecognized at the valuation date but were developed between the acquisition date and the test date. At the test date the fair values of the assets are deducted from the fair value of the reporting unit to determine the implied fair value of goodwill. If the implied fair value of goodwill at the test date is lower than its carrying amount, goodwill impairment is indicated and goodwill is written down to its implied fair value.[17] Performing the new asset allocation answers the implied question, "What exactly is impaired: specifically identifiable tangible assets, specifically identifiable intangible assets, or goodwill?" This is where SFAS No. 144 controls.

As stated in SFAS No. 142:

If goodwill and another asset (or asset group) of a reporting unit are tested for impairment at the same time, the other asset (or asset group) shall be tested for impairment before goodwill. For example, if a significant asset group is to be tested for impairment under Statement 121 [now 144] (thus potentially requiring a goodwill impairment test), the impairment test for the significant asset group would be performed before the goodwill impairment test. If the asset group was impaired, the impairment loss would be recognized prior to goodwill being tested for impairment.[18]

This means that impairment of other assets must also be recognized. Thus, the asset values recognized on the balance sheet as of the date of the impairment test will be the lower of the carrying value or fair value for each previously recognized tangible asset. For example, assume a company has a reporting unit with a fair value of $80,000,000 including goodwill of $35,000,000. Further assume that the relative fair values of the assets have been valued and recorded on the books of the acquirer as:

Recognized tangible assets	$15,000,000
Recognized identifiable intangible assets	
(with defined life)	30,000,000
Goodwill	35,000,000
Fair value of reporting unit	$80,000,000

After one year assume the carrying amount of certain assets after amortization are:

Recognized tangible assets	$12,000,000
Recognized identifiable intangible sssets	25,000,000

Now assume that an impairment test is performed at this time one year later and the fair value of the reporting unit is $70,000,000. This decline in value indicates impairment (step one fails) but not necessarily a goodwill impairment charge of $10,000,000. A new asset allocation (step two) must be performed to determine the new goodwill amount. The assumptions of the fair values as of the date of the impairment test are:

Recognized tangible assets	$13,000,000
Unrecognized tangible assets*	1,000,000
Recognized identifiable intangible assets	20,000,000
Unrecognized identifiable intangible assets*	7,000,000
Goodwill	29,000,000
Fair value of reporting unit	$70,000,000

*Assets acquired or developed after the acquisition date

The step two results are:

	Net Carrying Amount	Fair Value	Impairment Amount	SFAS Citation
Recognized tangible assets	$12,000,000	$13,000,000	$ 0	—
Unrecognized tangible assets	0	1,000,000	0	—
Recognized identifiable intangible assets				
(with a defined life)	25,000,000	20,000,000	5,000,000	144

Unrecognized identifiable intangible assets	0	7,000,000	0	—
Goodwill	35,000,000	29,000,000	6,000,000	142
Total	$72,000,000	$70,000,000	$11,000,000	

In this example, step one would fail by $2,000,000 (total carrying amount of $72,000,000 less fair value of $70,000,000), but the step two analysis shows required impairment expense of $11,000,000 ($5,000,000 under SFAS No. 144 and $6,000,000 under SFAS No. 142).

Of course, if the impairment test finds that the fair value of the reporting unit has not declined materially, no further analysis is required. *Increases* in goodwill value are never recognized.

TRANSITION: PREVIOUSLY RECOGNIZED GOODWILL

At the date SFAS No. 142 is initially applied, an entity must establish its reporting units using its current reporting structure and the reporting unit guidance from the Statement. Recognized net assets, excluding goodwill, should be assigned to those reporting units. Recognized assets and liabilities that do not relate to a reporting unit, such as an environmental liability for an operation previously disposed of, need not be assigned to a reporting unit. All goodwill recognized in an entity's statement of financial position should be assigned to one or more reporting units based on a reasonable and supportable analysis. Goodwill in each reporting unit should be tested for impairment as of the beginning of the fiscal year in which SFAS No. 142 is initially applied in its entirety. The amounts used in the transitional goodwill impairment test should be measured at the beginning of the year of initial application and the first step of the impairment test should be completed within six months of adoption. Further, if events or changes in circumstances indicate that the goodwill of a reporting unit might be impaired before completion of the transitional impairment test, goodwill should be tested for impairment when the impairment indicator arises. In addition to the transitional goodwill impairment test, an entity should perform the required annual goodwill impairment test in the year the Statement is adopted. That is, the transitional goodwill impairment test may not be considered the first year's annual test unless an entity designates the beginning of its fiscal year as of the date for its annual impairment test.[19]

Appendix 4.1

FINANCIAL REPORTING DISCLOSURES

The valuer must be aware of significant audit disclosures. For intangible assets subject to amortization the disclosures will include:

- The total amount assigned and the amount assigned to any major intangible asset class (see Exhibit 2.1)
- The amount of any significant residual value, in total and by major intangible assets class
- The weighted average amortization period, in total and by major intangible assets class[20]

For intangible assets not subject to amortization, the total amount assigned and the amount assigned to any major intangible asset class must be disclosed. Further, the amount of purchased in-process research and development assets acquired and written off in the period and the line item in the income statement in which the amount is written off or aggregated must be disclosed.[21]

For each period for which a statement of financial position is presented (i.e., each subsequent period to the acquisition) disclosure should include:

- The total gross carrying amount and accumulated amortization by major class for intangible assets subject to amortization
- Total amortization expense for the period
- The estimated aggregate amortization expense for each of the five succeeding fiscal years presented.[22]

For intangible assets not subject to amortization, the total carrying amount and the carrying amount for each major intangible asset class must be disclosed. Further, the changes in the carrying amount of goodwill during the period include:

- The aggregate amount of goodwill acquired
- The aggregate amount of impairment loss recognized

- The amount of goodwill included in the gain or loss on disposal of all or a portion of reporting unit[23]

Disclosure is more involved when an impairment loss is recognized. In such a situation, the following disclosures are required:

- A description of the facts and circumstances leading to the impairment
- The amount of the impairment loss and the method of determining the fair value of the associated reporting unit (whether based on quoted market prices, prices of comparable businesses, or a present value or other valuation technique)
- If a recognized impairment loss is an estimate that has not yet been finalized, that fact and the reasons for it should be disclosed. Further, in subsequent periods the nature and amounts of any significant adjustments made to the initial estimate of the impairment loss must be disclosed[24]

For goodwill, disclosures are required for the total amount of acquired goodwill and the amount that is expected to be deductible for tax purposes.[25] Further, the amount of goodwill allocated by reporting segment pursuant to FASB (SFAS No. 131, *Disclosures about Segments of Enterprise and Related Information*), should also be disclosed.[26] There are many other requirements for disclosure and the analyst is urged to work closely with the auditor in defining the scope of the valuation to assure all the elements of disclosure are included in the valuation report. Analysts must make sure their report and work papers provide the client and auditor the information necessary for these disclosures.

Chapter 5

Impairment Analysis: A Case Study

As described in the preceding chapter, under SFAS No. 142 goodwill is no longer amortized. Instead, goodwill is tested at least annually for impairment. The first step of the two-step impairment test, used to identify potential impairment, compares the fair value of the reporting unit with its carrying amount, including goodwill.[1] If the carrying value of the reporting unit exceeds its fair value, step two is triggered. The second step of the goodwill impairment test requires determining the amount of goodwill impairment associated with the impairment of the fair value of the reporting unit.[2] These two amounts will rarely be the same. All long-lived assets must be tested for impairment before the goodwill impairment test. This essentially implies a new purchase price allocation and it is likely that, if the fair value of the reporting unit is impaired, some of the recorded asset fair values may also be impaired.

In this chapter an impairment test is presented, assumed to be one year later, of the entity valued in Chapter 3. In this example, the reporting unit and the business enterprise are one and the same; thus the impairment test is done at the enterprise level. Larger companies will have multiple reporting units that must be separately analyzed. Our sample company is private, and we have determined that the best tool available is a discounted cash flow (DCF).

Obviously, the universe of acquired and acquirees is not limited to private companies. If the acquiring entity is public, the first thing management is going to look at is the stock price. Indeed, some managements have been criticized for spending too much time looking at their stock price! Certainly, a material decline in a company's stock price may indicate something is amiss and may be evidence enough to trigger step one of the impairment test—determining the *total impairment* of the reporting unit. Many public companies may observe a decline in their stock price between the two dates, but it is not sufficient to simply quantify the price decline of the stock and conclude that is the impairment amount. The reporting unit must be analyzed in detail to determine permanent impairment. A decline in the stock price may indicate something is wrong, but further analysis must be performed to determine how much, if any, of the impairment is permanent. Chapter 4 discusses the types of events that might indicate impairment of the fair value of the reporting unit. This example is presented to acquaint the reader with the mechanics of SFAS No. 142 impairment testing. While the initial triggers indicating step two may differ depending on whether the company is public or private (a material decline in the stock price for the former and an analysis of business fundamentals for the latter), the mechanics of impairment testing will be similar, with the primary difference being that private companies, lacking a readily ascertainable stock price, will place greater reliance on DCF or perhaps guideline company analyses for step one testing. For step two, both public and private company valuations will rely primarily on traditional methodologies such as the DCF.

Returning to the example, one area of inquiry is to compare 2002 actual with the 2002 forecast performed last year in conjunction with the purchase price analysis. As can be seen, actual operating results for 2002 lag well behind the forecast performed a year ago.

	2001 Actual	**2002 Forecast**	**2002 Actual**
Net sales	$60,000,000	$69,000,000	$56,000,000
Cost of sales	24,000,000	27,600,000	23,520,000
Cost of sales percentage	40.0%	40.0%	42.0%
Gross profit	$36,000,000	$41,400,000	$32,480,000
Operating expenses	18,000,000	20,700,000	17,360,000
EBITDA	18,000,000	20,700,000	15,120,000
EBITDA percentage	30.0%	30.0%	27.0%

While still profitable, the reporting unit's earnings before interest, taxes, depreciation, and amortization (EBITDA) was $15,120,000, 16 percent below 2001 actual EBITDA and 27 percent below the 2002 forecast. This information is evidence that the reporting unit's value likely is impaired, triggering step one of the impairment study—determining the fair value of the reporting unit and comparing that value with its carrying amount. If the carrying amount of a reporting unit exceeds its fair value, the second step of the goodwill impairment test is performed to measure the amount of goodwill impairment loss, if any.[3]

Now that we suspect that impairment exists, the challenge is to determine the fair value of the reporting unit as of the current date, December 31, 2002. Quoted market prices in active markets are considered the best evidence of fair value,[4] but the Statement allows that present value techniques are often the best. In our example, the carrying value of the reporting unit exceeds its fair value, triggering step two.

If a reporting unit fails step one, the interrelationship between SFAS Nos. 142 and 144, *Accounting for the Impairment or Disposal of Long-Lived Assets*, can be a little confusing and warrants comment. SFAS No. 144 states:

> An impairment loss shall be recognized only if the carrying amount of a long-lived asset (asset group) is not recoverable and exceeds its fair value. The carrying amount of a long-lived asset (asset group) is not recoverable if it exceeds the sum of the undiscounted cash flows expected to result from the use and eventual disposition of the asset (asset group).[5]

SFAS No. 144 provides guidance as to when to test for recoverability:

> A long-lived asset (asset group) shall be tested for recoverability whenever events or changes in circumstances indicate that its carrying amount may not be recoverable.[6]

If goodwill and other assets are tested for impairment at the same time, the other assets are to be tested for impairment before goodwill.[7]

The relatively poor financial performance described in our example would probably be reason enough to test the recoverability of long-lived assets under paragraphs 7 and 8 of SFAS No. 144. As will be seen later, the noncompete asset would pass and the technology asset would fail the recoverability test, which compares the asset's undiscounted cash flows with carrying values.

SFAS No. 144 contains similar language as SFAS No. 142 regarding the determination of fair value, stating a preference for quoted market prices but allowing other valuation techniques.[8] And in our example, and surely most other situations, quoted market prices for intangibles will not be available, requiring other techniques as would be developed in a SFAS No. 142 step two analysis.

Additionally, impairment testing of intangible assets not subject to amortization is covered by SFAS No. 142, not SFAS No. 144. In reality, while SFAS No. 142 requires, "If goodwill and another asset . . . are tested for impairment at the same time, the other asset . . . shall be tested before goodwill,"[9] impairment testing under SFAS Nos. 142 and 144 will be performed simultaneously in most cases. However, the final conclusion of goodwill will be determined subject to any revaluations of other assets.

As described in Chapter 3, a year ago the fair value of the assets of the reporting unit was determined to be $209,000,000. Now, after a year's depreciation, amortization (assuming MACRS-based depreciation for the depreciable tangible assets and straight-line amortization for the amortizable intangible assets), and the SFAS No. 2 charge for acquired in-process research and development, the carrying value of the assets of the reporting unit is $187,926,000. Allocated asset values are:

	12/31/01 Fair Value	12/31/02 Carrying Value
Cash	$ 1,500,000	$ 2,850,000
Investments in marketable securities	8,000,000	7,000,000
Accounts receivable	17,000,000	13,000,000
Inventory	12,000,000	10,500,000
Prepaid expenses	3,000,000	2,500,000
Total current assets	41,500,000	35,850,000
Land and buildings	22,000,000	21,687,000
Machinery and equipment, net	19,000,000	16,216,000
Total tangible assets	41,000,000	37,903,000
Software	7,070,000	5,300,000
Technology	13,500,000	10,120,000
In-process research and development	4,330,000	0
Trade name	23,760,000	23,760,000
Customer base	6,490,000	5,190,000
Noncompete agreement	9,300,000	7,440,000
Total intangible assets	64,450,000	51,810,000
Goodwill (including assembled workforce)	62,050,000	62,050,000
Total assets	$209,000,000	$187,613,000

To recap, for the impairment study, step one is to determine the overall fair value of the reporting unit and compare that value with its carrying value. If the carrying value of the reporting unit exceeds the new (current) fair value, impairment is indicated and we must then proceed to step two and determine the fair value of goodwill and other intangible assets (under SFAS Nos. 142 and 144).

BUSINESS ENTERPRISE VALUE

SFAS No. 142 requires that an analyst determine fair value first by looking at actual market prices of a company's stock. In this example, the company and reporting unit are the same. Since Target Company is privately held, no market prices or multiples are readily available. If the company were public, a material decline in the stock price would at least provide the rationale for performing further analysis in the step one test. But, as noted earlier, a decline in the stock price, while an indicator of the potential existence of impairment, likely will not by itself provide an accurate measure of permanent impairment. So, for public or private companies, further analysis will be necessary.

The next phase of the analysis is the performance of a business enterprise value (BEV) analysis as of December 31, 2002. The total fair value of the assets of the reporting unit comprises invested capital (as previously defined), plus current liabilities. Total assets of the reporting unit include current assets, tangible assets, intangible assets, and goodwill. The purpose of the new BEV is to determine the new fair values of invested capital and thus total assets (after adding non-interest-bearing liabilities) and to provide a framework for the revaluation of the other assets. SFAS No. 142 requires that the fair value of all of the assets of the reporting unit be determined as of the date of the impairment test. However, the only impairment adjustments actually recognized in the financial records are impairment of goodwill and of indefinitely lived intangible assets under SFAS No. 142 and impairment of other long-lived assets under SFAS No. 144. *The excess fair value over the carrying value of recognized intangibles and the fair values of previously unrecognized intangibles, while employed in the calculation of goodwill impairment, are not recorded in the final year-end accounting adjustments.* You can go down, but not up. We begin with a new DCF analysis as of December 31, 2002. The nature and underlying rationale for the DCF assumptions will be discussed throughout the chapter.

DISCOUNTED CASH FLOW APPROACH

In the discounted cash flow approach, a pro forma analysis is made of the subject company to estimate future available cash flows. *Available cash flow* is the amount that could be paid out to providers of capital without impairment of business operations.

Principal assumptions utilized in developing the estimates of cash flow are:

- As of December 31, 2002, the outlook is less bullish than a year ago. Sales are now forecast to increase from $56,000,000 in 2002 to $58,800,000 in 2003, representing growth of 5 percent, based largely on a decline in the growth rate in one of its key markets and a delay in completing the IPR&D project that was in process as of December 31, 2001. A year ago we were expecting double-digit growth for five years. The 10-year compound annual growth rate is forecast at 6.48 percent, down approximately 35 percent from the 10-year growth rate forecast a year ago.

- Operating margins before depreciation and amortization are forecast to decline to 27.5 percent in 2003, based on increased costs in 2002. Costs and expenses are expected to be brought back in line with last year's forecast by 2006. In this forecast, cost of sales and operating expenses exclude depreciation (tax—separately forecast using MACRS tables) and amortization.

- Working capital requirements (debt free) are still forecast at 15 percent of sales, based on the company's historical working capital position and projected needs.

- Capital expenditures are forecast at one percent of net sales. This level of capital expenditures is considered adequate to support future levels of sales.

- The tax amortization of total intangible asset value is a known quantity and remains the same as forecast last year. Section 197 of the Internal Revenue Code provides for such amortization over a 15-year period. The amortization acts as a tax shield and is added back to cash flow. Annual amortization is $8,433,000 ($126,500,000 ÷ 15, rounded). One year later, intangible asset amortization has a 14-year-remaining life, and the residual is adjusted accordingly (see Chapter 3 for a full discussion).[10] Remember, the example in Chapter 3 was of an asset purchase. In a stock purchase, the intangible assets generally would not be amortizable for tax purposes.

Other assumptions:

Required rate of return (discount rate)*	16.00%
Residual perpetual growth rate	5.00%
Tax rate	40.00%

*Discussed more fully in the "Discount Rate" section of this chapter.

Assumptions, as of December 31, 2002, are summarized in Exhibit 5.1, which presents the forecast cash flows for a period of 10 years.

Cash flows in 2012 were increased by the residual growth rate and then capitalized into perpetuity by the difference between the discount rate and the residual growth rate. This residual value was then discounted to present value to provide the net present value of the residual cash flow. The residual cash flow represents the expected cash flow for 2013 to perpetuity. The present value of the net cash flows, plus the present value of the residual growth rate, provides the total capitalized earnings. The BEV, as of December 31, 2002, is presented in Exhibit 5.2.

DISCOUNT RATE

The appropriate rate of return in valuing the enterprise is the weighted average cost of capital. This rate is typically the weighted average of the return on equity capital and the return on debt capital. The weights represent percentages of debt to total capital and equity to total capital. The rate of return on debt capital is adjusted to reflect the fact that interest payments are tax deductible to the corporation.

At December 31, 2002, the equity discount rate is assumed to be 20 percent, rounded, the same as last year (due to the rounding) and the pretax cost of debt 6 percent (borrowing rates generally have gone down). Substituting these values into the WACC formula described in Chapter 3 provides the following:

$$
\begin{aligned}
\text{WACC} &= (20.00\% \times 75.00\%) + (6.00\%[1 - 40.00\%] \times 25.00\%) \\
&= (15.00\%) + (3.60\% \times 25.00\%) \\
&= 15.00\% + 0.90\% \\
&= 15.90\%
\end{aligned}
$$

Rounded to, 16%

Exhibit 5.1 Target Company—Business Enterprise Value—Assumptions as of December 31, 2002 ($'000s)

| | ACTUAL | FORECAST | | | | | | | | | |
	2002	2003	2004	2005	2006	2007	2008	2009	2010	2011	2012
1. SALES											
Sales Growth Percentage		5.0%	10.0%	10.0%	8.0%	7.0%	5.0%	5.0%	5.0%	5.0%	5.0%
Net Sales	$56,000	$58,800	$64,680	$71,148	$76,840	$82,219	$86,330	$90,646	$95,178	$99,937	$104,934
2. EXPENSES											
Cost of Sales	$23,520	$24,696	$26,519	$28,459	$29,968	$32,065	$33,669	$35,352	$37,120	$38,976	$40,924
Cost of Sales Percentage	42.0%	42.0%	41.0%	40.0%	39.0%	39.0%	39.0%	39.0%	39.0%	39.0%	39.0%
Operating Expenses	$17,360	$17,934	$19,404	$21,344	$22,284	$23,843	$25,036	$26,287	$27,602	$28,982	$30,431
Operating Expenses Percentage	31.0%	30.5%	30.0%	30.0%	29.0%	29.0%	29.0%	29.0%	29.0%	29.0%	29.0%
Depreciation (MACRS)	$3,123	$3,112	$5,162	$3,927	$3,060	$2,456	$2,529	$2,607	$1,819	$1,016	$1,049
Other Income (Expense), net	0.0%	0.0%	0.0%	0.0%	0.0%	0.0%	0.0%	0.0%	0.0%	0.0%	0.0%
3. CASH FLOW											
Capital Expenditures		$588	$647	$711	$768	$822	$863	$906	$952	$999	$1,049
Capital Expenditures Percentage		1.0%	1.0%	1.0%	1.0%	1.0%	1.0%	1.0%	1.0%	1.0%	1.0%
Projected Working Capital as Percent of Sales		15.0%	15.0%	15.0%	15.0%	15.0%	15.0%	15.0%	15.0%	15.0%	15.0%
Projected Working Capital Balance (1)	$16,150	$8,820	$9,702	$10,672	$11,526	$12,333	$12,949	$13,597	$14,277	$14,991	$15,740
Projected Working Capital Requirement		(7,330)	882	970	854	807	617	647	680	714	750
4. OTHER											
Effective Tax Rate	40.0%	40.0%	40.0%	40.0%	40.0%	40.0%	40.0%	40.0%	40.0%	40.0%	40.0%
Required Rate of Return	16.0%										
Annual Amortization of Intangibles (Pretax) (2)	$8,433										

(1) Balance at December 31, 2002 stated at fair value.
(2) Calculated at time of acquistion: December 31, 2001

Note: Some amounts may not foot due to rounding.

The impairment test presented in this example is assumed to be performed as of December 31, 2002.

Exhibit 5.2 Target Company—Business Enterprise Value—Cash Flow Forecast as of December 31, 2002 ($'000s)

	ACTUAL 2002	FORECAST 2003	2004	2005	2006	2007	2008	2009	2010	2011	2012
Sales Growth Percentage		5.0%	10.0%	10.0%	8.0%	7.0%	5.0%	5.0%	5.0%	5.0%	5.0%
Net Sales	$56,000	$58,800	$64,680	$71,148	$76,840	$82,219	$86,330	$90,646	$95,178	$99,937	$104,934
Cost of Sales	23,520	24,696	26,519	28,459	29,968	32,065	33,669	35,352	37,120	38,976	40,924
Gross Profit	32,480	34,104	38,161	42,689	46,872	50,153	52,661	55,294	58,059	60,962	64,010
Operating Expenses	17,360	17,934	19,404	21,344	22,284	23,843	25,036	26,287	27,602	28,982	30,431
Depreciation (MACRS)	3,123	3,112	5,162	3,927	3,060	2,456	2,529	2,607	1,819	1,016	1,049
Amortization of Intangibles (Tax)	8,433	8,433	8,433	8,433	8,433	8,433	8,433	8,433	8,433	8,433	8,433
Total Operating Expenses	28,916	29,479	32,999	33,704	33,776	34,732	35,997	37,327	37,853	38,431	39,913
Taxable Income	3,564	4,625	5,162	8,985	13,096	15,421	16,664	17,967	20,205	22,531	24,097
Income Taxes	1,426	1,850	2,065	3,594	5,238	6,168	6,665	7,187	8,082	9,012	9,639
Net Income	$2,138	$2,775	$3,097	$5,391	$7,858	$9,253	$9,998	$10,780	$12,123	$13,518	$14,458
Net Cash Flow											
Net Income		$2,775	$3,097	$5,391	$7,858	$9,253	$9,998	$10,780	$12,123	$13,518	$14,458
Capital Expenditures		(588)	(647)	(711)	(768)	(822)	(863)	(906)	(952)	(999)	(1,049)
Change in Working Capital		7,330	(882)	(970)	(854)	(807)	(617)	(647)	(680)	(714)	(750)
Depreciation		3,112	5,162	3,927	3,060	2,456	2,529	2,607	1,819	1,016	1,049
Amortization of Intangibles (Tax)		8,433	8,433	8,433	8,433	8,433	8,433	8,433	8,433	8,433	8,433
Net Cash Flow		21,062	15,163	16,069	17,728	18,513	19,480	20,266	20,743	21,254	22,141
Present Value Factor, where Discount Rate = 16.0%		0.9285	0.8004	0.6900	0.5948	0.5128	0.4421	0.3811	0.3285	0.2832	0.2441
Present Value of Net Cash Flow		$19,555	$12,137	$11,088	$10,545	$9,493	$8,611	$7,723	$6,815	$6,019	$5,406

2012 Cash Flow	$22,141
Less: Tax Benefit of Amortization	(3,373)
2012 Cash Flow, net of Benefit	$18,768
2013 Cash Flow, Assuming Growth of 5.0%	$19,706
Residual Capitalization Rate	11.00%
Residual Value, 2013	$179,149
Present Value Factor	0.2441
Fair Value of Residual	$43,738
Net Present Value of Net Cash Flow, 2003–2012	$97,393
Net Present Value of Residual Cash Flow	43,738
Present Value of Amortization Tax Benefit, 2013–2016	2,304
Total Invested Capital, Rounded	$143,000

Amortization of Intangibles (Pretax)

	2013	2014	2015	2016
Amortization of Intangibles (Pretax)	8,433	8,433	8,433	8,433
Tax Benefit of Amortization	3,373	3,373	3,373	3,373
Present Value Factor	0.2105	0.1814	0.1564	0.1348
Present Value of Tax Benefit	$710	$612	$528	$455

Sum = Fair Value of Tax Benefit: $2,304

Note: Some amounts may not foot due to rounding.
The impairment test presented in this example is assumed to be performed as of December 31, 2002.

Applying the cost of capital to cash flows estimated earlier indicates the fair value of the invested capital of Target Company on the valuation date was $143,000,000 (Exhibit 5.2).

VALUATION OF CURRENT AND TANGIBLE ASSETS

Current Assets

As discussed in Chapter 3, the valuation of current assets requires cooperation between the analyst and auditor. Certain financial and other current assets are the province of the auditor, and the purchase price allocation should rely in part on audit conclusions for certain assets, such as cash and receivables. Marketable securities must be marked to market, often by simply obtaining brokerage statements. Previously recognized intangibles that represent capitalized historic expenditures, such as organization costs, are typically written off. The actual cash flow associated with these assets occurred in the past, and these assets typically cannot be separated or sold apart from the acquired entity as required under SFAS No. 141. Any other previously recorded intangible value is again subsumed in the current purchase price allocation.

The carrying values of the current assets as of December 31, 2002, are:

Asset	Carrying Value
Cash	$ 2,850,000
Marketable securities	7,000,000
Accounts receivable	13,000,000
Inventory	10,500,000
Prepaid expenses	2,500,000
Total current asset carrying value	$35,850,000

Fixed Assets

As has already been pointed out, very few business analysts have the experience and training to operate outside their disciplines to render valuation opinions on fixed assets. Usually, the real estate and personal property must be independently appraised. In this example, it is assumed that the real estate appraiser who determined the fair value of the land

and improvements to be $22,000,000 performed an update and the fair value as of December 31, 2002 is $23,000,000. The fair value of the machinery and equipment is assumed to remain unchanged at $19,000,000.

VALUATION OF INTANGIBLE ASSETS

Software

In reviewing the company's software system, there were two new modules developed in 2002, changing the total to 22 modules, each made up of a number of programs written in C++ programming language. The new line count is 332,980, up from 294,980 at December 31, 2001.

The next step is to determine the productivity with which the hypothetical recreation effort would take place. Again, management assessed a productivity rating of 1 to 3, with the same rates: Software rated 1 could be programmed at four lines of code per hour; software rated at 2 could be programmed at three lines of code per hour; and software rated 3, the most complex and difficult, could be programmed at two lines of code per hour.

Coding rates were assigned to the new modules and the calculation done as before. By dividing the lines of code by the coding rate, the number of hours to recreate totaled 126,840 hours for the entire system, up from 112,507 a year ago. The sum of hours was then multiplied by the blended hourly rate (fully burdened) of $125 per hour, an increase over the cost of $119 per hour calculated last year. *Reproduction cost* of the software system was determined by multiplying the total number of hours to recreate by the blended hourly rate. This amount totals $15,855,000.

If the software had been new as of the valuation date, the reproduction cost equates to brand-new software. As before, an obsolescence factor was applied to the reproduction cost to recognize the fact that the acquired software is not brand-new. Rather, it may have redundant or extraneous code and likely has been patched over the years and contains other inefficiencies that brand-new software presumably would not have. This year the obsolescence factor is estimated at 30 percent, as the continued aging of the old modules more than offsets the addition of the new modules. The obsolescence factor brings the *replacement cost* to $11,098,500. This value is then adjusted for taxes to recognize the deductibility of such expenses. The after-tax value is $6,659,100. Added to this amount is an amortization benefit, which reflects the additional value of the ability to deduct the amortization of the asset over its 15-year tax life (for fair value it is assumed the asset is bought in a *current* transaction[11] and amortized over a new 15-year period). Based on the cost approach, and after adjusting for taxes and amortization benefit, it was concluded that the fair value of the software as of December 31, 2002, was $7,810,000 (rounded) (Exhibit 5.3). One year later, the remaining useful life of the asset is three years.

Asset appreciation that may be determined during the course of an impairment analysis goes unrecognized. The fair value of Target Company's software is $7,810,000, which exceeds the carrying value of $5,300,000 ($7,070,000 less one year of straight-line amortization over a four-year life, rounded [see Exhibit 5.12] later in the chapter). The excess of the asset's fair value over its carrying value is not recognized. However, the current amount will be used internally to represent the fair value of the asset for the purpose of assessing contributory asset charges, which represent rental charges on certain intangible assets valued using the income approach.

Customer Base

To revalue the customer base as of December 31, 2002, the same cost approach methodology was used as employed last year (see Chapter 3 for a discussion of the cost and income approaches as they pertain to valuing a customer base). The total selling costs for the years ended December 31, 1999 to December 31, 2002 (there was an additional year's information as of the date of the impairment study) were calculated based on internally prepared financial statements and sales department detail, which was provided by management. In each year, the percentage of total revenue from new customers was determined. That percentage was applied to the company's total selling costs for each year to determine new customer selling cost.

These expenses were $61,100 in 2002, $123,246 in 2001, $119,938 in 2000, and $216,221 in 1999 for a total of $520,505 for the four years, during which 16 new customers were obtained. The after-tax selling costs were $312,303, or $19,519 per customer, determined by dividing after-tax selling costs by the 16 new customers obtained during the period. Multiplying the replacement cost per new customer times the 254 customers (a net decline of seven compared to last year) in the acquired customer base as of the date of the impairment study provides a replacement cost of the customer base of $4,957,826. No obsolescence is recognized for this asset. The amortization benefit is

Exhibit 5.3   Target Company—Valuation of Acquired Software as of December 31, 2002 ($'000s)

All software was developed internally by Company for its own use. Rights to software were transferred at acquisition.

The software is written in C++ programming language.

Valuation is based on cost to replace less obsolescence. Costs are based on internally developed Company metrics for software development productivity.

Source: Leonard Riles, Director of Product Development

IN PLACE	LINES OF CODE	PRODUCTIVITY RATING (1)	RATE (1)	HOURS TO RECREATE
Module 1	26,400	2	3.0	8,800
Module 2	32,600	3	2.0	16,300
Module 3	46,000	1	4.0	11,500
Module 4	8,480	3	2.0	4,240
Module 5	12,000	3	2.0	6,000
Module 6	12,500	2	3.0	4,167
Module 7	2,000	2	3.0	667
Module 8	32,000	2	3.0	10,667
Module 9	3,000	2	3.0	1,000
Module 10	3,000	2	3.0	1,000
Module 11	3,000	2	3.0	1,000
Module 12	13,000	2	3.0	4,333
Module 13	6,000	2	3.0	2,000
Module 14	10,000	2	3.0	3,333
Module 15	5,000	2	3.0	1,667
Module 16	6,000	2	3.0	2,000
Module 17	5,000	3	2.0	2,500
Module 18	8,000	1	4.0	2,000
Module 19	7,000	2	3.0	2,333
Module 20	54,000	3	2.0	27,000
Module 21	10,000	3	2.0	5,000
Module 22	28,000	2	3.0	9,333

Total Number of Lines	332,980			
Total Number of Hours to Recreate				126,840
Times: Blended Hourly Rate (see below)				$125
Reproduction Cost				$15,855,000
Less: Obsolescence (2)		30.0%		(4,756,500)
Replacement Cost				$11,098,500
Less: Taxes @		40.0%		(4,439,400)
After-Tax Value Before Amortization Benefit				$6,659,100
Amortization Benefit				
Discount Rate		18.0%		
Tax Rate		40.0%		
Tax Amortization Period		15		
Amortization Benefit				1,152,068
Fair Value of Software, Rounded				$7,810,000

(1) Lines of code per hour, based on productivity assessment for average module of programming.
(2) Estimate based on number of lines of redundant/extraneous code and effective age and remaining economic lives of system.

SOFTWARE DEVELOPMENT COSTS - ESTIMATED PROJECT TEAM

FUNCTION	NUMBER	BURDENED HOURLY RATE
Project Manager	1	$ 210.00
Systems Analyst	2	160.00
Technical Writer	1	130.00
Programmer	4	120.00
Support	2	55.00
Blended Hourly Rate, Rounded		$125.00

Note: Some amounts may not foot due to rounding.

The impairment test presented in this example is assumed to be performed as of December 31, 2002.

Exhibit 5.4   Target Company—Valuation of Customer Base as of December
31, 2002

HISTORICAL CUSTOMER DATA

YEAR	TOTAL SELLING COSTS	PERCENT OF REVENUE FROM NEW CUSTOMERS	NEW CUSTOMER SELLING COSTS	NUMBER OF NEW CUSTOMERS
2002	$6,500,000	0.94%	$61,100	3
2001	5,010,000	2.46%	123,246	4
	5,307,000	2.26%	119,938	5
1999	4,848,000	4.46%	216,221	4
	$21,665,000		$520,505	16

CALCULATION OF FAIR VALUE

Total Pretax Selling Costs - New Customers		$520,505
Less: Taxes @	40.0%	(208,202)
After Tax Selling Costs - New Customers		$312,303
Divided by: Number of New Customers, 1999—2002		16
Replacement Cost per New Customer		$19,519
Times: Number of Acquired Customers		254
Replacement Cost of Customer Base		$4,957,826
Amortization Benefit		
Discount Rate	18.0%	
Tax Rate	40.0%	
Tax Amortization Period	15	
Amortization Benefit		857,736
Fair Value of Customer Base, Rounded		$5,820,000

Note: Some amounts may not foot due to rounding.
The impairment test presented in this example is assumed to be performed as of December 31, 2002.

$857,736. Thus, the fair value of the customer base as of December 31,
2002, was $5,820,000 (rounded) (Exhibit 5.4). The fair value exceeds
the asset's carrying value of $5,190,000 (see Exhibit 5.12 later in the
chapter), but the increase is not recorded in the financial statements.
The remaining useful life is now four years.

Assembled Workforce

The buyer of Target Company obtained an assembled and trained
workforce of 65 employees. As of the date of the impairment test,
headcount reductions had reduced the assembled workforce to 54 em-

ployees. As before, the cost approach (assemblage cost avoided) was employed to value this asset. Using this method, the costs associated with employee recruitment, selection, and training provide the measurement of value.

Recruiting costs are incurred to obtain a new employee; as before, the average recruiting cost is 27.5 percent of starting salary. The training costs of an employee reflect the amount of time inefficiently used by a

Exhibit 5.5   Target Company—Valuation of Assembled Workforce as of December 31, 2002

NO.	JOB TITLE	SALARY	20% BENEFITS	TOTAL	(1) TRAIN. PER. CL.	YRS.	33.3% COST	(2) 27.5% RECRUIT.	INTERVIEW & H.R.	TOTAL
1	Member of Technical Staff	$90,000	$18,000	$108,000	1	0.125	$4,500	$24,750	$375	$29,625
2	Member of Technical Staff	44,953	8,991	53,944	1	0.125	2,248	12,362	375	14,985
3	Member of Operations Staff	71,641	14,328	85,969	1	0.125	3,582	19,701	375	23,658
4	Account Executive	91,170	18,234	109,404	1	0.125	4,559	25,072	375	30,006
5	Member of Technical Staff	107,888	21,578	129,466	2	0.375	16,183	29,669	750	46,602
6	Member of Technical Staff	33,244	6,649	39,893	1	0.125	1,662	9,142	375	11,179
7	Vice President	142,000	28,400	170,400	2	0.375	21,300	39,050	750	61,100
8	Member of Technical Staff	83,647	16,729	100,376	2	0.375	12,547	23,003	750	36,300
9	Member of Operations Staff	104,700	20,940	125,640	1	0.125	5,235	28,793	375	34,403
10	Chief Architect	155,500	31,100	186,600	3	0.750	46,650	42,763	1,500	90,913
11	Director of Development	135,000	27,000	162,000	2	0.375	20,250	37,125	750	58,125
12	Member of Technical Staff	77,772	15,554	93,326	2	0.375	11,666	21,387	750	33,803
13	Account Executive	94,950	18,990	113,940	1	0.125	4,748	26,111	375	31,234
14	Member of Technical Staff	81,300	16,260	97,560	1	0.125	4,065	22,358	375	26,798
15	Chief Executive Officer	250,000	50,000	300,000	1	0.125	12,500	68,750	375	81,625
16	Member of Technical Staff	82,000	16,400	98,400	2	0.375	12,300	22,550	750	35,600
17	Member of Technical Staff	57,460	11,492	68,952	1	0.125	2,873	15,802	375	19,050
18	Account Executive	106,400	21,280	127,680	2	0.375	15,960	29,260	750	45,970
19	Member of Technical Staff	107,867	21,573	129,440	2	0.375	16,180	29,663	750	46,593
20	Member of Technical Staff	110,000	22,000	132,000	3	0.750	33,000	30,250	1,500	64,750
21	Vice President of American Sales	135,000	27,000	162,000	2	0.375	20,250	37,125	750	58,125
22	Member of Technical Staff	114,500	22,900	137,400	1	0.125	5,725	31,488	375	37,588
23	Member of Technical Staff	47,028	9,406	56,434	1	0.125	2,351	12,933	375	15,659
24	Account Executive	90,660	18,132	108,792	1	0.125	4,533	24,932	375	29,840
25	Member of Technical Staff	63,329	12,666	75,995	1	0.125	3,166	17,415	375	20,956
26	Member of Operations Staff	131,000	26,200	157,200	1	0.125	6,550	36,025	375	42,950
27	Chief Financial Officer	150,000	30,000	180,000	1	0.125	7,500	41,250	375	49,125
28	Member of Technical Staff	100,210	20,042	120,252	2	0.375	15,032	27,558	750	43,340
29	Member of Technical Staff	87,372	17,474	104,846	2	0.375	13,106	24,027	750	37,883
30	Director of Operations	137,000	27,400	164,400	3	0.750	41,100	37,675	1,500	80,275
31	Member of Technical Staff	94,248	18,850	113,098	2	0.375	14,137	25,918	750	40,805
32	Member of Operations Staff	71,000	14,200	85,200	1	0.125	3,550	19,525	375	23,450
33	Director of Marketing	125,000	25,000	150,000	2	0.375	18,750	34,375	750	53,875
34	Member of Technical Staff	65,000	13,000	78,000	1	0.125	3,250	17,875	375	21,500
35	Member of Technical Staff—Nonexempt	42,950	8,590	51,540	1	0.125	2,148	11,811	375	14,334
36	Member of Technical Staff	90,000	18,000	108,000	1	0.125	4,500	24,750	375	29,625
37	Member of Technical Staff	109,000	21,800	130,800	2	0.375	16,350	29,975	750	47,075
38	Member of Technical Staff	84,200	16,840	101,040	1	0.125	4,210	23,155	375	27,740
39	Member of Technical Staff	60,300	12,060	72,360	1	0.125	3,015	16,583	375	19,973
40	Member of Technical Staff	58,500	11,700	70,200	1	0.125	2,925	16,088	375	19,388
41	Director Release & Customer Support	116,000	23,200	139,200	2	0.375	17,400	31,900	750	50,050
42	Executive Assistant	35,000	7,000	42,000	1	0.125	1,750	9,625	375	11,750
43	Member of Technical Staff	113,400	22,680	136,080	2	0.375	17,010	31,185	750	48,945
44	Member of Technical Staff	112,041	22,408	134,449	2	0.375	16,806	30,811	750	48,367
45	Member of Operations Staff	70,000	14,000	84,000	1	0.125	3,500	19,250	375	23,125
46	Member of Technical Staff	107,000	21,400	128,400	3	0.750	32,100	29,425	1,500	63,025
47	Director of International Operations	150,000	30,000	180,000	1	0.125	7,500	41,250	375	49,125
48	Member of Technical Staff	110,000	22,000	132,000	2	0.375	16,500	30,250	750	47,500
49	Vice President and General Manager of EMEA	145,000	29,000	174,000	2	0.375	21,750	39,875	750	62,375
50	Account Executive	82,500	16,500	99,000	1	0.125	4,125	22,688	375	27,188
51	Account Executive	75,261	15,052	90,313	2	0.375	11,289	20,697	750	32,736
52	Member of Technical Staff	67,735	13,547	81,282	2	0.375	10,160	18,627	750	29,537
53	Member of Technical Staff	73,350	14,670	88,020	2	0.375	11,003	20,171	750	31,924
54	Member of Technical Staff	99,465	19,893	119,358	3	0.750	29,840	27,353	1,500	58,693
Total 54		$5,240,541	$1,048,108	$6,288,649			$644,889	$1,441,151	$34,125	$2,120,165

			Replacement Cost of Assembled Workforce		$2,120,165
			Less: Taxes	40.0%	(848,066)
		Interview & H.R.	Costs Avoided, Net of Tax		$1,272,099
(1) Qualified Replacement Training Months	Hours	Rate	Amortization Benefit		
1 = < 3 months	5	$75.00	Rate of Return	16.0%	
2 = 3-6 months	10	$75.00	Tax Rate	40.0%	
3 = 6-12 months	20	$75.00	Tax Amortization Period	15	
(2) Source: Karl Malloney, Recruiter			Amortization Benefit		242,543
			Fair Value of Assembled Workforce, Rounded		$1,510,000

Note: Some amounts may not foot due to rounding.
The impairment test presented in this example is assumed to be performed as of December 31, 2002.

new employee (inefficiency training cost) and the time inefficiently used by a training supervisor (direct training cost) during the first few months on the job. Training costs were estimated by multiplying the fully burdened weekly salary of the employee or supervisor by the average amount of inefficiency incurred during the training period. The inefficiency estimate remains at 33.3 percent. Interview costs were estimated in the same manner as last year's analysis (shown in Chapter 3).

The summation of the hiring and training costs results in the total cost to replace the assembled workforce are summarized in Exhibit 5.5. Based on the cost approach, and after adjusting for taxes at 40 percent and adding an amortization benefit, the fair value of the assembled workforce is estimated to be $1,510,000 (rounded) at December 31, 2002. No obsolescence is recognized for this asset (Exhibit 5.5).

SFAS No. 141 specifically prohibits the recognition of assembled workforce as an intangible asset apart from goodwill. However, in the application of the excess earnings approach, which is used to value Target Company's technology and in-process research and development, "returns on" are taken on the fair values of all of the contributory assets acquired in the acquisition. The value of the assembled workforce is calculated so that such a return may be taken. However, its fair value is included in goodwill in the final allocation of purchase price.

Trade Name

As discussed earlier, Target Company has one valuable trade name. All of the company's products and services are sold under the X trade name, and each major product is identified by this trade name.

The relief from royalty method was employed. A royalty rate of four percent is again applicable, stated as a percentage of sales. Applying this same rate to a lower sales forecast obviously results in a lower fair value as of December 31, 2002.

The rights to use the trade name transfer to the buyer in perpetuity, giving it an indefinite life. The fair value of the trade name is the present value of the royalties forecast for the five-year period of 2003 to 2007, plus the present value of the residual at the end of the five-year period, plus the amortization benefit. A 16 percent rate of return was again chosen to reflect a risk assessment that the trade name was about as risky as the business overall. Based on the analysis as presented in Exhibit 5.6, the fair value of the trade name as of the valuation date was $18,450,000. The carrying value is $23,760,000 (see Exhibit 5.12 later

Exhibit 5.6   Target Company—Valuation of Trade Name as of December 31, 2002 ($'000s)

		2003	2004	2005	2006	2007
Net Sales from Business Enterprise Valuation (1)		$58,800	$64,680	$71,148	$76,840	$82,219
Pretax Relief from Royalty	4.0%	$2,352	$2,587	$2,846	$3,074	$3,289
Income Tax Liability	40.0%	941	1,035	1,138	1,229	1,315
After-Tax Royalty		1,411	1,552	1,708	1,844	1,973
Present Value Income Factor	16.0%	0.9285	0.8004	0.6900	0.5948	0.5128
Present Value Relief from Royalty		$1,310	$1,242	$1,178	$1,097	$1,012
Sum of Present Value Relief from Royalty, 2003-2007		$5,840				
Residual Calculation:						
2007 After-Tax Royalty		$1,973				
2008 After-Tax Royalty, Assuming Growth of	5.0%	$2,072				
Residual Capitalization Rate		11.0%				
Residual Value, 2008		$18,833				
Present Value Factor		0.5128				
Fair Market Value of Residual		9,657				
Present Value of Trade Name Royalty Flows		15,497				
Amortization Benefit						
Discount Rate	16.0%					
Tax Rate	40.0%					
Tax Amortization Period	15					
Amortization Benefit		2,955				
Fair Value of Trade Name, Rounded		$18,450				
(1) Figures shown from Business Enterprise Valuation (Exhibit 5.2)						

Note: Some amounts may not foot due to rounding.
The impairment test presented in this example is assumed to be performed as of December 31, 2002.

in the chapter). This indefinitely lived intangible asset is impaired and will be written down to its new fair value.

Noncompete Agreement

In the interest of brevity and because we already have a full BEV analysis as an example, assume that under the assumption of competition, the seller could negatively impact Target Company, affecting the growth of sales (i.e., the seller, if not under a noncompete agreement, could theoretically go to work for a competitor or start a new company and cause Target Company to grow more slowly than otherwise forecast) and causing it to incur more marketing and other expenses. The same rate of return was used as for the BEV, 16 percent. The resulting BEV without a noncompete agreement in place is $136,000,000. Thus, as shown in Exhibit 5.7, the value of the noncompete agreement is:

	Invested Capital
BEV with agreement in place (rounded)	$143,000,000
BEV without agreement in place	$136,000,000
Difference equals gross value of agreement	$ 7,000,000

Exhibit 5.7 Target Company—Valuation of Noncompete as of December 31, 2002 ($'000s)

| | ACTUAL | FORECAST | | | | | | | | | | |
	2002	2003	2004	2005	2006	2007	2008	2009	2010	2011	2012
Sales Growth Percentage (1)		2.5%	5.0%	10.0%	8.0%	7.0%	5.0%	5.0%	5.0%	5.0%	5.0%
Net Sales	$56,000	$57,400	$60,270	$66,297	$71,601	$76,613	$80,443	$84,466	$88,689	$93,123	$97,780
Cost of Sales Percentage (1)	42.0%	42.0%	41.0%	40.0%	39.0%	39.0%	39.0%	39.0%	39.0%	39.0%	39.0%
Cost of Sales	$23,520	$24,108	$24,711	$26,519	$27,924	$29,879	$31,373	$32,942	$34,589	$36,318	$38,134
Gross Profit	32,480	33,292	35,559	39,778	43,676	46,734	49,071	51,524	54,100	56,805	59,646
Operating Expense Percentage (1)	31.0%	32.0%	31.0%	30.0%	29.0%	29.0%	29.0%	29.0%	29.0%	29.0%	29.0%
Operating Expenses	$17,360	$18,368	$18,684	$19,889	$20,764	$22,218	$23,329	$24,495	$25,720	$27,006	$28,356
Depreciation (MACRS)	3,123	3,112	5,162	3,927	3,060	2,456	2,529	2,607	1,819	1,016	1,049
Amortization of Intangibles (Tax)	8,433	8,433	8,433	8,433	8,433	8,433	8,433	8,433	8,433	8,433	8,433
Total Operating Expenses	28,916	29,913	32,279	32,249	32,257	33,107	34,291	35,535	35,972	36,455	37,838
Taxable Income	3,564	3,379	3,281	7,529	11,420	13,627	14,780	15,989	18,129	20,350	21,808
Income Taxes	1,426	1,352	1,312	3,012	4,568	5,451	5,912	6,396	7,251	8,140	8,723
Net Income	$2,138	$2,028	$1,968	$4,518	$6,852	$8,176	$8,868	$9,593	$10,877	$12,210	$13,085
Net Cash Flow											
Net Income		$2,028	$1,968	$4,518	$6,852	$8,176	$8,868	$9,593	$10,877	$12,210	$13,085
Capital Expenditures		(574)	(603)	(663)	(716)	(766)	(804)	(845)	(887)	(931)	(978)
Change in Working Capital		7,540	(431)	(904)	(796)	(752)	(575)	(603)	(633)	(665)	(698)
Depreciation		3,112	5,162	3,927	3,060	2,456	2,529	2,607	1,819	1,016	1,049
Amortization of Intangibles (Tax)		8,433	8,433	8,433	8,433	8,433	8,433	8,433	8,433	8,433	8,433
Net Cash Flow		20,538	14,530	15,310	16,833	17,547	18,451	19,185	19,609	20,063	20,890
Present Value Factor, where Discount Rate = 16.0%		0.9285	0.8004	0.6900	0.5948	0.5128	0.4421	0.3811	0.3285	0.2832	0.2441
Present Value of Net Cash Flow		$19,069	$11,630	$10,564	$10,013	$8,998	$8,156	$7,311	$6,442	$5,682	$5,100

Note: Some amounts may not foot due to rounding.
The impairment test presented in this example is assumed to be performed as of December 31, 2002.

		2013	2014	2015	2016
2012 Cash Flow	$20,890				
Less: Tax Benefit of Amortization	(3,373)				
2012 Cash Flow, net of Benefit	$17,517	Amortization of Intangibles (Pretax)	$8,433	$8,433	$8,433	$8,433
2013 Cash Flow, Assuming Growth of	5.0% 18,393					
Residual Capitalization Rate	11.00%	Tax Benefit of Amortization	3,373	3,373	3,373	3,373
		Present Value Factor	0.2105	0.1814	0.1564	0.1348
Residual Value, 2013	$167,207					
Present Value Factor	0.2441	Present Value of Tax Benefit	$710	$612	$528	$455
Fair Value of Residual	$40,823					
		Sum = Fair Value of Tax Benefit	$2,304			
Net Present Value of Net Cash Flow, **2003–2012**	$92,966					
Net Present Value of Residual Cash Flow	40,823					
Present Value of Amortization Tax Benefit, 2013–2016	2,304					
Total Invested Capital **with Competition**, Rounded	$136,000					
Business Enterprise Value (Exhibit 5.2)	143,000					
Difference = Gross Value of Noncompete	$7,000					
Times: Probability Factor (2)	60.0%					
Probability Adjusted Value of Noncompete	$4,200					
Amortization Benefit						
Discount Rate	16.0%					
Tax Rate	40.0%					
Amortization Period	15					
Amortization Benefit	800					
Fair Value of Noncompete Agreement, Rounded	$5,000					

(1) Percentages based on assumption of competition. See discussion in **Noncompete** Section of Chapter 5.
(2) To account for likelihood of competing absent an agreement and likelihood of success.

						FORECAST					
	2003	2004	2005	2006	2007	2008	2009	2010	2011	2012
SFAS No. 144 Impairment Test										
Undiscounted Net Cash Flows, BEV (Exhibit 5.2)	$21,062	$15,163	$16,069	$17,728	$18,513	$19,480	$20,266	$20,743	$21,254	$22,141
Undiscounted Net Cash Flows, BEV with Competition	20,538	14,530	15,310	16,833	17,547	18,451	19,185	19,609	20,063	20,890
Difference = Net Cash Flows, Attributable to Noncompete	$524	$633	$759	$895	$965	$1,029	$1,081	$1,135	$1,191	$1,251

Sum of Net Cash Flows, Attributable to Noncompete $9,463
Carrying Value of Noncompete $7,440

Conclusion: Recoverable under SFAS No. 144, therefore no impairment.

Note: Some amounts may not foot due to rounding.
The impairment test presented in this example is assumed to be performed as of December 31, 2002.

The probability of the covenantor's competing and succeeding is still assessed at 60 percent. After reducing the gross value by the probability factor and adding an amortization benefit, the fair value of the noncompete agreement is determined to be $5,000,000.

The recoverability test of SFAS No. 144 indicates that the sum of the undiscounted cash flows (here, for 10 years, ignoring the residual) exceeds the carrying value. Thus, no impairment is recognized. The remaining useful life is now four years.

Technology

As was done last year, the fair value of the company's developed technology was determined using an income approach, which measures the present value of the future earnings to be generated during the remaining lives of the assets. Using the BEV as a starting point, pretax cash flows attributable to the technology that existed at the valuation date were calculated. This was accomplished by management's forecasting sales attributable to the existing technology. These sales were estimated to decline in 2003, remain flat in 2004, increase two percent in 2005, and grow at three percent per year thereafter. As with the BEV, deductions are made for cost of goods sold (42 percent of sales attributable to existing technology in 2003, 41 percent in 2004, and 40 percent thereafter) and operating expenses (normalized at 19 percent in 2006, after deducting development expenses [again, 10 percent] from the base to reflect the fact that the developed technology should not be burdened by expenses of developing new technology). We then adjusted for returns on the other identified assets. Contributory asset charges (discussed more fully in Chapter 3) are as follows:

Return on

Working capital	5.0%
Land and building	7.0%
Machinery and equipment	8.0%
Software	18.0%
Trade name	16.0%
Noncompete agreement	16.0%
Assembled workforce	16.0%
Customer base	18.0%

Required returns were deducted from the cash flows from the BEV. The contributory charges are presented in Exhibit 5.8.

Exhibit 5.8 Target Company—Valuation of Technology as of December 31, 2002 ($'000s)

CALCULATION OF CONTRIBUTORY ASSET CHARGES

Contributory Asset

A. Asset Balances		2003	2004	2005	2006	2007
Net Working Capital		$12,485	$9,261	$10,187	$11,099	$11,929
Land and Buildings		22,919	22,764	22,621	22,490	22,367
Machinery and Equipment, net		17,819	14,455	10,732	8,110	6,270
Software		7,810	7,810	7,810	7,810	7,810
Trade Name		18,450	18,450	18,450	18,450	18,450
Noncompete Agreement		5,000	5,000	5,000	5,000	0
Assembled Workforce		1,510	1,510	1,510	1,510	1,510
Customer Base		5,820	5,820	5,820	5,820	5,820

B. Total Returns	Rate	2003	2004	2005	2006	2007
Net Working Capital	5.0%	$624	$463	$509	$555	$596
Land and Buildings	7.0%	1,604	1,593	1,583	1,574	1,566
Machinery and Equipment, net	8.0%	1,426	1,156	859	649	502
Software	18.0%	1,406	1,406	1,406	1,406	1,406
Trade Name	16.0%	2,952	2,952	2,952	2,952	2,952
Noncompete Agreement	16.0%	800	800	800	800	0
Assembled Workforce	16.0%	242	242	242	242	242
Customer Base	18.0%	1,048	1,048	1,048	1,048	1,048

C. Distribution of Revenues	2003	2004	2005	2006	2007
Technology	$50,400	$50,400	$51,408	$52,950	$54,539
IPR&D	8,400	14,280	19,740	23,890	27,680
Total DCF Revenues	$58,800	$64,680	$71,148	$76,840	$82,219
Technology Percent	85.71%	77.92%	72.26%	68.91%	66.33%
IPR&D Percent	14.29%	22.08%	27.74%	31.09%	33.67%
Total	100.00%	100.00%	100.00%	100.00%	100.00%

D. Allocated Returns—Technology	2003	2004	2005	2006
Net Working Capital	$535	$361	$368	$382
Land and Buildings	1,375	1,242	1,144	1,085
Machinery and Equipment, net	1,222	901	620	447
Software	1,205	1,095	1,016	969
Trade Name	2,530	2,300	2,133	2,034
Noncompete Agreement	686	623	578	551
Assembled Workforce	207	188	175	166
Customer Base	898	816	757	722
Total	$8,658	$7,527	$6,791	$6,357

E. Allocated Returns—IPR&D	2003	2004	2005	2006	2007
Net Working Capital	$89	$102	$141	$173	$201
Land and Buildings	229	352	439	489	527
Machinery and Equipment, net	204	255	238	202	169
Software	201	310	390	437	473
Trade Name	422	652	819	918	994
Noncompete Agreement	114	177	222	249	0
Assembled Workforce	35	53	67	75	81
Customer Base	150	231	291	326	353
Total	$1,443	$2,133	$2,608	$2,868	$2,798

Note: Some amounts may not foot due to rounding.

The impairment test presented in this example is assumed to be performed as of December 31, 2002.

We then reevaluated a study related to the expected life of the technology, which produced a survivor curve based on a four-year remaining useful life, during which the asset is forecast to function at 100 percent (i.e., no economic deterioration) in 2003, 90 percent in 2004, 60 percent in 2005, and 40 percent productivity in year four. The surviving cash flows (the excess cash flows multiplied by the forecast survivorship of the technology in each year), after providing for returns on the other assets, are attributable to the technology. The discount rate of 18 percent reflects the higher risk of this asset compared with the business overall.

Exhibit 5.9　　Target Company—Valuation of Technology as of December 31, 2002 ($'000s)

		ACTUAL	FORECAST			
		2002	2003	2004	2005	2006
			-10.0%	0.0%	2.0%	3.0%
Net Sales—Existing Technology (1)		$56,000	$50,400	$50,400	$51,408	$52,950
Cost of Sales		23,520	21,168	20,664	20,563	20,651
Gross Profit		32,480	29,232	29,736	30,845	32,300
Operating Expenses (2)		11,760	10,332	10,080	10,282	10,061
Depreciation		3,123	2,667	4,022	2,837	2,108
Total Operating Expenses		14,883	12,999	14,102	13,119	12,169
Taxable Income		17,597	16,233	15,634	17,726	20,131
Income Taxes		7,039	6,493	6,254	7,090	8,052
Net Income		$10,558	$9,740	$9,380	$10,635	$12,078
Residual Cash Flow Attributable to Technology						
Less Returns on						
$16,150	Net Working Capital	5.0%	$535	$361	$368	$382
23,000	Land and Buildings	7.0%	1,375	1,242	1,144	1,085
19,000	Machinery and Equipment, net	8.0%	1,222	901	620	447
7,810	Software	18.0%	1,205	1,095	1,016	969
18,450	Trade Name	16.0%	2,530	2,300	2,133	2,034
5,000	Noncompete Agreement	16.0%	686	623	578	551
1,510	Assembled Workforce	16.0%	207	188	175	166
5,820	Customer Base	18.0%	898	816	757	722
	Sum of Returns		$8,658	$7,527	$6,791	$6,357
	After-Tax Residual Cash Flows		$1,082	$1,853	$3,845	$5,721
	Survivorship of Technology (3)		100.0%	90.0%	60.0%	40.0%
	Surviving Residual Cash Flows (4)		$1,082	$1,668	$2,307	$2,289
18.00%	Present Value Factor for Residual Cash Flow		0.9206	0.7801	0.6611	0.5603
	Present Value of Surviving Residual Cash Flows		$996	$1,301	$1,525	$1,282
	SFAS No. 144 Impairment Test					
	Sum of Undiscounted Residual Cash Flows (4)		$7,345			
	Sum of Present Values, 2003–2006		$5,104			
	Amortization Benefit					
	Discount Rate	18.0%				
	Tax Rate	40.0%				
	Tax Amortization Period	15				
	Amortization Benefit		883			
	Fair Value of Technology, Rounded		$5,990			

(1) Based on 2002 actual sales, with growth attritutable to existing technology.
(2) Excludes development expenses of 10 percent to reflect that developed technology should not be burdened by expenses of developing new technology.
(3) Assumes 4 year life.
(4) The sum of the undiscounted, cash flows of $7,345 is less than the carrying value of $10, 120, indicating

Note: Some amounts may not foot due to rounding.
The impairment test presented in this example is assumed to be performed as of December 31, 2002.

Based on our analysis, we concluded that the fair value of the acquired technology on the valuation date was $5,990,000 (rounded), as shown in Exhibit 5.9. The recoverability test of SFAS No. 144 indicates that the sum of the undiscounted cash flows is less than the carrying value. Thus, the asset is considered impaired and will be written down to its new fair value. The remaining useful life of the revalued asset is four years.

In-Process Research and Development

The value of the in-process research and development was also estimated using the income approach. Similarly to our methodology for valuing technology, the discounted cash flow model was constructed starting with expected sales based on the technology that was in process at the valuation date. In this example, it is assumed that the IPR&D that was being developed as of the date of the impairment study was delayed, contributing to the company's decline in performance, and it is now scheduled to be completed in early 2003 and is forecast to produce sales of $8,400,000. Sales are further forecast to increase rapidly in subsequent years.

Similar to the technology valuation, cost of sales and operating expenses (net of development costs, which will no longer occur relative to this technology) are deducted. We reevaluated the expected survivorship pattern, and the useful life of the IPR&D is now estimated to be five years, during which the technology is forecast to function at 100 percent for the first year, then decline in productivity to 90 percent in 2004, 70 percent in 2005, 60 percent in 2006, and 30 percent in 2007. In addition, estimated required returns were taken on the contributory assets (see previous section), except for existing technology (see discussion in Chapter 3). Although the forecast survivorship "roll-off" of the IPR&D spans a five-year period, a return on the noncompete agreement stops after four years, its remaining useful life (the contractual life of December 31, 2001, was five years). This is because, unlike the other assets, the noncompete agreement is not replenished or renewed through ongoing expenditures, and it has no value when its contractual life is over. This is generally true for nonrenewable contractual assets.

The sum of the present values is $2,076,000. A discount rate of 25 percent was selected to reflect the additional risk of the unproven technology. After accounting for the amortization benefit, the fair value of the IPR&D (as shown in Exhibit 5.10) as of December 31, 2002, was $2,350,000.

The fair value of acquired IPR&D was written off in 2002 under SFAS No. 2. The fair value of IPR&D concluded herein will be used in

Exhibit 5.10 Target Company—Valuation of In-Process Research and Development as of December 31, 2002 ($'000s)

			FORECAST		
	2003	2004	2005	2006	2007
Net Sales—New Technology (1)	$8,400	$14,280	$19,740	$23,890	$27,680
Cost of Sales	3,528	5,855	7,896	9,317	10,795
Gross Profit	4,872	8,425	11,844	14,573	16,885
Operating Expenses (2)	1,722	2,856	3,948	4,539	5,259
Cost to Complete	240	0	0	0	0
Depreciation	445	1,140	1,090	951	827
Total Operating Expenses	2,407	3,996	5,038	5,490	6,086
Taxable Income	2,465	4,430	6,806	9,082	10,799
Income Taxes	986	1,772	2,723	3,633	4,319
Net Income	$1,479	$2,658	$4,084	$5,449	$6,479

Residual Cash Flow Attributable to Technology

Less Returns on							
$16,150	Net Working Capital	5.0%	$89	$102	$141	$173	$201
23,000	Land and Building	7.0%	229	352	439	489	527
19,000	Machinery and Equipment, net	8.0%	204	255	238	202	169
7,810	Software	18.0%	201	310	390	437	473
18,450	Trade Name	16.0%	422	652	819	918	994
5,000	Noncompete Agreement	16.0%	114	177	222	249	0
1,510	Assembled Workforce	16.0%	35	53	67	75	81
5,820	Customer Base	18.0%	150	231	291	326	353
	Sum of Returns		$1,443	$2,133	$2,608	$2,868	$2,798
	After-Tax Residual Cash Flows		$36	$525	$1,476	$2,581	$3,681
	Survivorship of Technology (3)		100.0%	90.0%	70.0%	60.0%	30.0%
	Surviving Excess Cash Flows		$36	$473	$1,033	$1,549	$1,104
25.0%	Present Value Factor for Residual Cash Flow		0.8944	0.7155	0.5724	0.4579	0.3664
	Present Value of Surviving Residual Cash Flows		$32	$338	$592	$709	$405

Sum of Present Values, 2003–2007		$2,076
Amortization Benefit		
Discount Rate	25.0%	
Tax Rate	40.0%	
Tax Amortization Period	15	
Amortization Benefit		270
Fair Value of IPR&D Rounded		$2,350

(1) Based on Business Enterprise Value (Exhibit 5.2), less sales due to existing Technology (Exhibit 5.9).
(2) Excludes development expenses of 10 percent to reflect no future developement costs relative to this technology.
(3) Assume 5 year life.

Note: Some amounts may not foot due to rounding.
The impairment test presented in this example is assumed to be performed as of December 31, 2002.

the determination of goodwill impairment but will not be recognized: The carrying value of IPR&D will continue to be zero.

Valuation of Goodwill

Again, goodwill is calculated using the residual method, by subtracting from the purchase price the fair value of all the identified tangible and intangible assets. Remember, goodwill includes assembled workforce but assembled workforce must be separately valued to obtain a valid return for IPR&D and technology. As a result and pursuant to SFAS No. 141, the indicated value of assembled workforce of $1,510,000 must be added

Exhibit 5.11   Target Company—Valuation of Goodwill as of December 31, 2002 ($'000s)

Total Value of Invested Capital	$143,000
Debt-Free Current Liabilities	20,000
Total Liabilities and Equity	163,000
Less: Fair Value of Current Assets	(36,150)
Less: Fair Value of Tangible Assets	(42,000)
Less: Fair Value of Intangible Assets	
Software	(7,810)
Customer Base	(5,820)
Trade Name	(18,450)
Noncompete Agreement	(5,000)
Technology	(5,990)
In-Process Research and Development	(2,350)
Residual Goodwill	$39,430

Note: Some amounts may not foot due to rounding.
The impairment test presented in this example is assumed to be performed as of December 31, 2002.

to the indicated value of goodwill to arrive at the fair value of goodwill for financial statement reporting purposes.

Based on this analysis, the fair value of residual goodwill on December 31, 2002, was $39,430,000 (Exhibit 5.11).

CONCLUSION

As the fair value of goodwill has declined from $62,050,000 to $39,430,000, an impairment loss is recognized in the amount of $22,620,000. Other assets indicating impairment are:

	Carrying Value before Impairment 12/31/02	Fair Value 12/31/02	Impairment YE 12/31/02
Trade name (SFAS No. 142)	$23,760,000	$18,450,000	$5,310,000
Technology (SFAS No. 144)	10,120,000	5,990,000	4,130,000
Total	$33,880,000	$24,440,000	$9,440,000

Exhibit 5.12 Target Company—Summary of Fair Values and Impairment Losses as of December 31, 2002 ($'000s)

	FAIR VALUE 12/31/01	CARRYING VALUE BEFORE IMPAIRMENT 12/31/02	FAIR VALUE 12/31/02	CARRYING VALUE AFTER IMPAIRMENT 12/31/02	IMPAIRMENT 12/31/02
Cash	$1,500	$2,850	$2,850	$2,850	na
Investments in Marketable Securities	8,000	7,000	7,300	7,000	na
Accounts Receivable	17,000	13,000	13,000	13,000	na
Inventory	12,000	10,500	10,500	10,500	na
Prepaid Expenses	3,000	2,500	2,500	2,500	na
TOTAL CURRENT ASSETS	41,500	35,850	36,150	35,850	0
Land and Buildings	22,000	21,687	23,000	21,687	0
Machinery and Equipment, net	19,000	16,216	19,000	16,216	0
TOTAL LONG-LIVED TANGIBLE ASSETS	41,000	37,903	42,000	37,903	0
TOTAL CURRENT AND TANGIBLE ASSETS	82,500	73,753	78,150	73,753	0
Software	7,070	5,300	7,810	5,300	0
Technology	13,500	10,120	5,990	5,990	(4,130)
In-Process Research and Development	4,330	0	2,350	0	0
Trade Name	23,760	23,760	18,450	18,450	(5,310)
Customer Base	6,490	5,190	5,820	5,190	0
Noncompete Agreement	9,300	7,440	5,000	7,440	0
TOTAL IDENTIFIED INTANGIBLE ASSETS	64,450	51,810	45,420	42,370	(9,440)
GOODWILL (including assembled workforce)	62,050	62,050	39,430	39,430	(22,620)
TOTAL ASSETS	$209,000	$187,613	$163,000	$155,553	($32,060)

Note: Some amounts may not foot due to rounding.

The impairment test presented in this example is assumed to be performed as of December 31, 2002.

The short-lived assets are not subject to impairment review. In the case of software, customer base, and in-process research and development, the fair values as of December 31, 2002, exceed their carrying values. No adjustments are made to reflect valuation differences. A summary of the impairment study is presented in Exhibit 5.12. Total impairment losses for 2002 are $32,060,000.

Chapter 6

Issues in and Implementation of SFAS Nos. 141 and 142

The FASB's issuance of SFAS Nos. 141 and 142 initiates a movement toward consistency in financial statement reporting that will take time to fully implement. The FASB recognizes this and has scheduled a number of clarifications and projects designed to provide additional clarity. For example, the Board declared that the phrase *accounting records have been maintained* as used in footnote 25 to paragraph 61(b) of SFAS No. 141 is intended to mean that an entity is accounting for an acquired intangible asset separately from goodwill as evidenced by the maintenance of separate general ledger accounts, subsidiary ledgers, or spreadsheets for that intangible asset to which it posted periodic amortization charges, impairment charges, and any other accounting entries related to that asset.[1]

In addition, the Board stated that, except for the amount recognized as an excess reorganization in accordance with AICPA Statement of Position 90-7, *Financial Reporting by Entities in Reorganization Under the Bankruptcy Code*, SFAS No. 142 does not change the accounting for specific intangible assets provided by GAAP. For example, SFAS No. 142 does not change the requirement to amortize recognized film cost assets (whether acquired in a business combination or by other means) in accordance with AICPA Statement of Position 00-2, *Accounting by Producers or Distributors of Films*.[2]

A number of other issues are being addressed by formal projects under the Board's authority. The issues fall into seven topics:

1. Purchase method procedures
2. Treatment of intangible asset value subsumed

3. Defining reporting units
4. Negative goodwill (equity method)
5. New basis accounting
6. Disclosure of internally generated intangible assets
7. Business combinations of not-for-profit organizations

PURCHASE METHOD PROCEDURES

The treatment for preacquisition contingencies is essentially grandfathered from APB Opinion No. 16 (paragraph 88) and shall govern the purchase price allocation if the contingency can be resolved during the allocation period. If the contingency cannot be clearly resolved, then it will still be included in the allocation to the degree the contingency can be reasonably estimated. Preacquisition contingencies are a hotbed of controversy, particularly with regard to the determination of the cost of an acquisition, the determination of direct versus indirect acquisition costs, contingent compensation for services, as well as others. The FASB has announced a project to address the purchase method, specifically preacquisition contingencies. Until such a project results in a new Statement, the practitioner needs to consider the following guidance (not all inclusive):

- SFAS No. 5, *Accounting for Contingencies*
- FASB Interpretation No. 14, *Reasonable Estimation of the Amount of Loss*
- Emerging Issues Task Force (EITF) Issue No. 95-8, *Accounting for Contingent Consideration Paid to the Shareholders of an Acquired Enterprise in a Purchase Business Combination*
- EITF Issue No. 97-8, *Accounting for Contingent Consideration Issued in a Purchase Business Combination*
- EITF Issue No. 97-15, *Accounting for Contingency Arrangements Based on Security Prices in a Purchase Business Combination*
- EITF Issue No. 99-12, *Determination of the Measurement Date for the Market Price of Acquirer Securities Issued in a Purchase Business Combination*
- EITF Topic No. D-87, *Determination of the Measurement Date for Consideration Given by the Acquirer in a Business Combination When That Consideration Is Securities Other Than Those Issued by the Acquirer*

The FASB project, *Business Combinations: Purchase Method Procedures* (the Project), is a joint project with the International Accounting Standards Board (IASB) and will broadly reconsider aspects of the purchase method of accounting, including measuring the value of the business combination, and recognition and measurement of identifiable assets and liabilities (including such issues as contingencies and liabilities for terminating activities of an acquired entity). As reported by the FASB, some of the decisions tentatively agreed upon are:

1. The accounting for a business combination is based on the assumption that the transaction is an exchange of equal values; the total amount to be recognized should be measured based on the fair value of the consideration paid or the fair value of the net assets acquired, whichever is more clearly evident.
   - If the consideration paid is cash or other assets (or liabilities incurred) of the acquiring entity, the fair value of the consideration paid determines the total amount to be recognized in the financial statements of the acquiring entity.
   - If the consideration is in the form of equity instruments, the fair value of the equity instruments ordinarily is more clearly evident than the fair value of the net assets acquired and, thus, will determine the total amount to be recognized by the acquiring entity.
2. In a business combination, the acquiring entity obtains control over the acquired entity and is therefore responsible for the assets and liabilities of the acquired entity. An amount equal to the fair value, on the date control is obtained, should be assigned to the identifiable assets acquired and liabilities assumed.
   - If the total fair value exchanged in the purchase transaction exceeds the amounts recognized for identifiable net assets, that amount is the *implied* fair value of goodwill.
   - If the total fair value exchanged in the purchase transaction is less than the amounts recognized for identifiable net assets, that amount should be recognized as a gain in the income statement.
3. In the acquisition of less than 100 percent of the acquired entity, the identifiable assets and liabilities of the acquired entity should be recorded at full fair value. The current practice of considering the subsidiaries' carryover basis to the extent of the noncontrolling interest should be eliminated.
4. If negative goodwill is present in a business combination, the acquiring entity should review the procedures used to identify and measure

the net assets of the subsidiary; however, no asset acquired should be measured at an amount that is known to be less than its fair value, nor should any liability assumed or incurred be measured at an amount known to be higher than its fair value. If negative goodwill remains, the acquiring entity should recognize the amount in the income statement (recognized as an extraordinary item under Statement 141).

5. Preacquisition contingencies of the acquired entity that are assets or liabilities should be recognized and should be initially measured at fair value. The Board agreed to eliminate the alternative described in paragraph 40(b) of Statement 141 that allows for recognition under an approach consistent with FASB Statement No. 5, *Accounting for Contingencies*. The issue of measuring preacquisition contingencies subsequent to the acquisition date will be addressed in the project at a later date.[3]

At its March 6, 2002, meeting, the Board continued deliberations on the Project on Business Combinations—Purchase Method Procedures. The Board discussed the accounting for contingent consideration in a business combination. The Board reached the following tentative decisions:

- Contingent consideration issued in a business combination is an obligation of the acquirer as of the acquisition date and therefore should be recognized as part of the purchase price on that date. Consistent with the working principle, the initial measurement of contingent consideration should be at fair value.

- Some contingent consideration arrangements obligate the acquirer to deliver its equity securities if specified future events occur. Presuming that the Board issues a standard on accounting for financial instruments with the characteristics of liabilities, equity, or both, prior to the issuance of guidance in this project, the guidance in that standard would apply to contingent consideration arrangements.

- The exception in paragraph 11(c) of FASB Statement No. 133, *Accounting for Derivative Instruments and Hedging Activities*, should be eliminated in order that contingent consideration arrangements that otherwise meet the definition of a derivative would be subject to the requirements of Statement 133.

- Subsequent remeasurement (after the acquisition date) of contingent consideration liabilities does not result in a change to the purchase price of the business combination. These amounts therefore should be recorded in the income statement.[4]

TREATMENT OF SUBSUMED INTANGIBLE ASSET VALUE

In an impairment study, if original goodwill includes identified but previously unrecorded intangible assets, an important question arises. Are previously unrecorded intangibles to be valued so they may provide an appropriate contributory charge? It would seem this step is necessary to ensure all of the intangibles are properly valued and the residual value applicable to goodwill is accurate. Or, should previously unrecorded intangibles not be valued based on the argument that the goodwill that was calculated in prior periods considered only recorded assets? Such an approach would result in no allocation of contributory charges, thereby overstating certain assets. Such overstatement would be offset by ignoring the previously unrecorded assets in calculating the residual value that equates to goodwill. In any event, goodwill would likely be incorrect as a result.

The Board has taken the position that, in determining the amount of goodwill impairment, all economic assets should be valued and appropriate returns assessed, regardless of whether these assets are recorded as of the date of the impairment study. The reader is cautioned that this procedure is specific to the calculation of goodwill for the impairment measurement. In no circumstances are previously unrecorded intangibles to be later recorded in the financial statements. This conclusion follows from the requirement that sufficient records exist for the accurate valuation of the intangible asset. Absent the existence of such records, it would not be possible to value such intangible assets. These conclusions are addressed in an FASB Staff Announcement, Topic No. D-100, which is reprinted in its entirety in Exhibit 6.1 at the end of this chapter.

DEFINING REPORTING UNITS

What are the criteria for defining a component of an operating segment as a reporting unit? Should there be geographic distinction, even though the economic purpose of the component is similar? Should the Board allow the maximization of rollups of reporting units? The staff of the FASB has addressed these issues by focusing on:

• Whether the component constitutes a business
• Availability of discrete financial information

- Accountability of segment management
- Existence of similar economic characteristics

As stated in the FASB staff announcement (Topic No. D-101, reproduced in its entirety in Exhibit 6.2 at the end of this chapter),

> Components that share similar economic characteristics but relate to different operating segments may not be combined into a single reporting unit. For example, an entity might have organized its operating segments on a geographic basis. If its three operating segments (Americas, Europe, and Asia) each have two components (A & B) that are dissimilar to each other but similar to the corresponding components in the other operating segment, the entity would *not* be permitted to combine component A from each of the operating segments to make reporting unit A.[5]

NEGATIVE GOODWILL (EQUITY METHOD)

What has come to be known as *negative goodwill* (a popular oxymoron, but preferable to *badwill*) is to be eliminated through an exercise that applies a pro-rata reduction of the negative goodwill amount to the previously determined asset values. SFAS No. 141 states:

> In some cases, the sum of the amount assigned to assets acquired and liabilities assumed will exceed the cost of the acquired entity (excess over cost or excess). That excess shall be allocated as a pro-rata reduction of the amounts that otherwise would have been assigned to all of the acquired assets except (a) financial assets other than investments accounted for by the equity method, (b) assets to be disposed of by sale, (c) deferred tax assets, (d) prepaid assets relating to pension or other postretirement benefit plans, and (e) any other current assets.
>
> If any excess remains after reducing to zero the amounts that otherwise would have been assigned to those assets, that remaining excess shall be recognized as an extraordinary gain as described in paragraph 11 of APB Opinion No. 30, *Reporting the Results of Operations—Reporting the Effects of Disposal of a Segment of a Business, and Extraordinary, Unusual and Infrequently Occurring Events and Transactions.*[6]

Goodwill resulting from the equity method is to be grandfathered. As SFAS No. 142 states:

The portion of the difference between the cost of an investment and the amount of underlying equity in that asset of an equity method investee that is recognized as goodwill in accordance with paragraph 19(b) of APB Opinion No. 18, *The Equity Method of Accounting for Investments and Common Stock* (equity method goodwill) shall not be amortized. However, equity method goodwill shall not be tested for impairment in accordance with this statement [SFAS No. 142]. Equity method investment shall continue to be reviewed for impairment in accordance with paragraph 19(h) of Opinion 18.[7]

Paragraph 19(h) of APB Opinion No. 18, *The Equity Method of Accounting for Investments in Common Stock*, states:

A loss in value of an investment that is other than a temporary decline should be recognized the same as a loss in value of other long-term assets. Evidence of a loss in value might include, but would not necessarily be limited to, absence of an ability to recover the carrying amount of the investment or inability of the investee to sustain earnings capacity, which would justify the carrying amount of the investment. A current fair value of an investment that is less than its carrying amount may indicate a loss in value of the investment. However, a decline in the quoted market price below the carrying amount or the existence of operating losses is not necessarily indicative of a loss in value that is other than temporary. All are factors to be evaluated.[8]

Following the logic of APB Opinion No. 18 and SFAS No. 142, goodwill on the investee's balance sheet will be subject to the new rules while the investor will be required under the equity method to recognize its share of impairment losses recognized by the investee. Further, if the investee subsequently recognizes goodwill impairment, the investor under the equity method should consider whether its carrying value of the investee is likewise impaired.

NEW BASIS ACCOUNTING

The FASB (in cooperation with the IASB) has announced a separate project which:

. . . focuses on those situations in which fresh-start (a new basis at fair value) recognition and measurement of all of an entity's assets and liabilities would be appropriate. One commonly identified candidate for application of this approach would be a multiparty business combination or other new entity formation in which no single pre-existing entity obtains majority ownership and control of the resulting new entity. Similarly, joint venture formations also are candidates for this accounting treatment. Related issues include the recognition and measurement of goodwill and other intangibles in combinations or other transactions accounted for by the fresh-start method.

Prior to its designation as a potential IASB/FASB joint project, the Board, at its September 13, 2000 meeting, formally approved the initial focus of Business Combinations: Phase 2 on new basis accounting issues. The Board also approved a draft working principle to be utilized in the determination of the appropriateness of recognizing a new basis of accounting. The Board decided that the scope of the project should include the issue of gain recognition in the financial statements of the entity that has transferred control over net assets to a joint venture.

During the fourth quarter 2000, the Board discussed the recognition of a new basis of accounting in connection with the formation of a joint venture. The Board decided that a change in control over net assets from unilateral control by one entity to joint or shared control by that entity and one or more other entities should result in a new basis of accounting for those net assets in the financial statements of the jointly controlled entity. The Board also discussed gain recognition, as of the date of formation of a joint venture, in the financial statements of an investor that transfers an appreciated (or previously unrecognized) asset to the joint venture. The Board decided that an entity that exchanges appreciated (or previously unrecognized) assets for an equity interest in a joint venture should recognize a gain on the assets exchanged.[9]

INTERNALLY GENERATED INTANGIBLE ASSETS

The FASB is currently undertaking a project that will review the disclosure of intangible assets that are not recognized in statements of financial position, but would have been recognized if acquired either separately or in a business combination. Generally known as *internally generated goodwill*, the subjects of the project will include in-process research and development and focus on qualitative as well as quantitative issues. The project is ongoing, with an exposure draft expected in the third quarter of 2002. The project proposal is reproduced in its entirety in Exhibit 6.3 at the end of this chapter.

BUSINESS COMBINATIONS
FOR NOT-FOR-PROFIT ORGANIZATIONS

The FASB is studying the application of SFAS Nos. 141 and 142 to not-for-profit (NFP) organizations, which were originally excluded from those Statements. The project will follow an approach that presumes that Statement No. 141 should apply to combinations of NFP organizations unless a circumstance unique to those combinations is identified that would justify a different accounting treatment. That approach is being referred to as the *differences-based approach*. The definition of NFP originally and in SFAS No. 116, *Accounting for Contributions Received and Contributions Made* (June 1993), continue while the scope of the project will include combinations between two or more NFP organizations and the acquisition of a for-profit business enterprise by an NFP organization. The acquisition of an NFP organization by a business enterprise is within the scope of SFAS No. 141. The project analyzing NFPs will also include accounting for combinations of two or more mutual enterprises.

As part of the project, the Board has made tentative decisions regarding the accounting for a combination of two NFP organizations in which the acquiring organization can be identified and no cash or other assets are exchanged as consideration:

- A combination of that type should be accounted for by the acquiring organization in a manner similar to a contribution under SFAS No. 116. The contribution should be measured as the sum of the fair values of the identifiable assets acquired and the liabilities assumed. The assets acquired and liabilities assumed should initially be recognized at their fair values, and the excess of the sum of the fair values of the identifiable assets acquired over the sum of the fair values of the liabilities assumed should be recognized as a contribution received.
- In those rare cases in which the sum of the fair values of the liabilities assumed exceeds the sum of the fair values of the identifiable assets acquired, the acquiring organization should initially recognize that excess as an unidentifiable intangible asset (goodwill).[10]

The Board made the following decisions regarding the accounting for a combination of NFP organizations in which cash or other assets are exchanged as consideration. The decisions apply to both combinations between two or more NFP organizations as well as the acquisition of a business enterprise by an NFP organization:

- The combination should be accounted for by the acquiring organization in accordance with Statement 141. However, the facts and circumstances surrounding the combination should be reviewed to assess whether the combination is a transaction that is in part an exchange and in part a contribution. If the facts and circumstances provide clear evidence that there is a contribution inherent in the transaction, that contribution received should be recognized by the acquiring organization in accordance with Statement 116. The following are examples of facts and circumstances that provide evidence that the combination is one that is in part an exchange and in part a contribution:
  a. The sum of the fair values of the assets acquired and liabilities assumed exceeds the fair value of the consideration exchanged (the excess), particularly if the amount of that excess is substantial in relation to the fair value of the net assets acquired, and no unstated rights or privileges are involved.
  b. A review of the facts and circumstances surrounding the combination, including careful study of the negotiations, provides evidence that the participants were acting as a donor and a donee and as buyer and a seller.
- Organizations should be provided with the following list of examples of facts and circumstances that indicate a combination is a bargained exchange:
  a. The organization or business enterprise is acquired through a competitive bidding process involving multiple potential acquirers.
  b. The amount of consideration offered by the acquiring organization was developed in consultation with acquisition advisors, was based on an estimate of the acquired entity's fair value, or both. That estimate of the acquired entity's fair value may have been developed internally by the acquiring organization or by independent valuation experts.
  c. The acquired entity's former parent or predecessor board of directors retained outside specialists to assist in negotiating the combination, used estimates of the organization's fair value to evaluate the adequacy of the offers received, or both.
  d. One or both parties to the combination retained consultants to provide an opinion on the fairness of the transaction.

e. The provisions of NFP corporation law or involvement on the part of a state attorney general or other regulatory body influenced the terms or structure of the combination transaction.

- If the acquired entity is an NFP organization, the contribution inherent in a combination should be measured as the excess of the sum of the fair values of the identifiable assets acquired and the liabilities assumed (following the guidance in paragraph 37 of Statement 141) over the fair value of the consideration exchanged.

- If the acquired entity is a business enterprise, the contribution inherent in a combination should be measured as the excess of the fair value of the acquired business enterprise over the cost of that business enterprise.

- Contingent consideration in a combination should be accounted for in accordance with the guidance in Statement 141.

- In general, assets transferred or liabilities incurred by the acquiring organization as a requirement of a combination should be accounted for as consideration paid for the acquired entity unless the acquiring organization retains control over the future economic benefits of the transferred assets. If control over the future economic benefits of the transferred assets is retained by the acquiring organization, the asset transfer should be reported as an asset-for-asset exchange. Examples of conditions that would result in the acquiring organization retaining control over the future economic benefit or the transferred assets include:
  a. The asset transfer is repayable or refundable.
  b. The assets are transferred to a recipient that is controlled by the acquiring organization.
  c. The assets are transferred with the stipulation that they be used on behalf of, or for the benefit of, the acquired organization, the acquiring organization, or its affiliates.

- An acquiring NFP organization should account for a regulatory-required asset transfer as consideration paid for the acquired organization.

- Communities neither own nor control NFP organizations and, therefore, a community's relationship with an NFP organization should have no effect on the method of accounting for a combination of NFP organizations.[11]

CONCLUSION

As can be seen, the FASB is grappling with a number of correlary issues. We believe the subsequent development of the decision will result in the completion of the logical framework. It is imperative that the practitioner closely monitor the development and resolution of subsequent decisions.

Exhibit 6.1 FASB Staff Announcement—Topic No. D-100

Topic: Clarification of Paragraph 61(b) of FASB Statement No. 141 and Paragraph 49(b) of FASB Statement No. 142

Date Discussed: November 14–15, 2001

An FASB representative announced that the staff has received inquiries about the application of paragraph 61(b) of FASB Statement No. 141, *Business Combinations*, and paragraph 49(b) of FASB Statement No. 142, *Goodwill and Other Intangible Assets*. The interpretative guidance provided by this staff announcement was formally cleared by the Board at its October 10, 2001 meeting.

Paragraph 61 of Statement 141 includes the following transition provisions:

The following transition provisions apply to business combinations for which the acquisition date was before July 1, 2001, that were accounted for using the purchase method:

a. The carrying amount of acquired intangible assets that do not meet the criteria in paragraph 39 for recognition apart from goodwill (and any related deferred tax liabilities if the intangible asset is not deductible for tax purposes) shall be reclassified as goodwill as of the date Statement 142 is initially applied in its entirety.

b. The carrying amount of (1) any recognized intangible assets that meet the recognition criteria in paragraph 39 or (2) any unidentifiable intangible assets recognized in accordance with paragraph 5 of FASB Statement No. 72, *Accounting for Certain Acquisitions of Banking or Thrift Institutions*, that have been included in the amount reported as goodwill (or as goodwill and intangible assets) shall be reclassified and accounted for as an asset apart from goodwill as of the date Statement 142 is initially applied in its entirety.[25]

c. Other than as set forth in (a) and (b), an entity shall not change the amount of the purchase price assigned to the assets acquired and liabilities assumed in a business combination for which the acquisition date was before July 1, 2001. [Footnote 26 omitted.]

---

[25]For example, when a business combination was initially recorded, a portion of the [cost of the] acquired entity was assigned to intangible assets that meet the recognition criteria in paragraph 39. Those intangible assets have been included in the amount reported on the statement of financial position as goodwill (or as goodwill and other intangible assets), however, separate general ledger or other accounting records have been maintained for those assets.

November 14–15, 2001 EITF Meeting Minutes, p. 1   Administrative Matters

Exhibit 6.1   *(Continued)*

The FASB staff has received inquiries about the application of subparagraph 61(b) (the Transition Provision), in particular, the meaning of *assigned to* and *accounting records have been maintained for those assets* as those phrases are used in the footnote to the Transition Provision. The following paragraphs summarize the FASB staffs understanding of the Board's intent with respect to the Transition Provision and provide examples to illustrate its application.

During the development of the Transition Provision, the Board noted that "entities might not have adhered strictly to the purchase price allocation requirements in Opinion 16 because Opinion 17 required amortization of all acquired intangible assets and limited the maximum amortization period for both goodwill and other intangible assets to 40 years" (footnote 36 to paragraph B220 of Statement 141). The Board believes that many entities concluded that their financial statements were prepared in accordance with generally accepted accounting principles, in all material respects, even though intangible assets acquired in a business combination were not recognized and accounted for separately from goodwill. In those cases, the FASB staff believes that the Transition Provision does not allow those entities to "carveout" from goodwill any intangible assets they had not identified and measured at fair value in the initial recording of a business combination and subsequently accounted for separately from goodwill. Rather, the FASB staff believes it was the Board's intent to require reclassification of the carrying amount of a previously acquired intangible asset only if (a) the asset meets the recognition criteria in paragraph 39 of Statement 141, (b) the asset had been assigned an amount equal to its estimated fair value at the date that the business combination was initially recorded, and (c) the asset was accounted for separately from goodwill as evidenced by the maintenance of accounting records for that asset, such as a separate general ledger or other subsidiary ledgers (such as a spreadsheet or similar ledger account) to which periodic amortization charges, impairment charges, and other accounting entries were posted.

The following examples illustrate the staffs understanding of how the Transition Provision should be applied.

Case A
In recording the acquisition of a bank, the acquiring entity identified the core deposit intangible (CDI) asset as an acquired intangible asset, estimated its fair value at date of acquisition, determined its useful life, and recognized deferred taxes related to that asset. The acquiring entity combined the CDI asset and goodwill into a single amount for external reporting purposes and that combined amount was recorded in a single general ledger account labeled goodwill and other intangible assets. However, separate subsidiary ledgers (in the form of spreadsheets) were maintained for goodwill and for the CDI asset to which periodic amortization and impairment charges were posted.

The FASB staff believes that the acquirer is required by the Transition Provision to reclassify the carrying amount of the CDI asset to an account other than goodwill as of the date Statement 142 is adopted in its entirety. The CDI asset meets the recognition criteria in paragraph 39 of Statement 141, its fair value was measured at the date [of] acquisition, and separate accounting records were maintained for the asset. The FASB staff believes that after adoption of Statement 142, the separate CDI asset should continue to be amortized over its remaining useful life.

November 14–15, 2001 EITF Meeting Minutes, p. 2   Administrative Matters

Exhibit 6.1 *(Continued)*

Case B

In recording the acquisition of a bank, the acquiring entity identified a CDI asset as an acquired intangible asset and estimated its fair value at date of acquisition. The acquiring entity decided, however, to recognize the CDI asset and goodwill as a single asset labeled goodwill and to amortize that combined asset over its estimated composite useful life of 15 years. The acquiring entity reasonably concluded that the financial reporting results produced by amortizing the combined amount recognized as goodwill over its composite useful life would not be materially different from the results that would have been produced had the CDI asset been recognized and accounted for separately from goodwill. At the date the combination was completed, the acquiring entity recorded the amounts assigned to goodwill and to the CDI asset in a single general ledger account. In subsequent periods, accounting records were maintained only for the combined asset. The acquiring entity has, however, retained in its accounting records documentation supporting the initial recording of the business combination that includes information about the estimated fair value of the acquired CDI asset and its useful life.

The FASB staff believes that the Transition Provision does not permit *the acquiring entity to change the amount of the purchase price assigned to goodwill because, in this case, while the acquirer had identified and estimated the fair value of the CDI asset at the date that the business combination was initially recorded, separate accounting records (such as a separate general ledger account or spreadsheet)* were not *maintained for the asset.*

Additional Observations

While the above examples refer to a particular type of intangible asset, a core deposit intangible asset of an acquired financial institution, the FASB staff believes that the interpretative guidance in this staff announcement applies to *all* intangible assets acquired in past business combinations, including those with indefinite useful lives.

The FASB staff believes that for a business combination completed after June 30, 2001, the approach described in Case B (that is, subsuming an acquired CDI asset into the amount recognized as goodwill when recording a business combination) would be inconsistent with the requirements of Statement 141. That is because the staff believes that a CDI asset meets the criteria in paragraph 39 of Statement 141 for recognition as an asset apart from goodwill.

The FASB staff also observes that the amount of future goodwill impairment losses recognized might be affected if an acquired intangible asset is not reclassified and accounted for apart from goodwill on transition to Statement 142. That is because the goodwill impairment loss would be measured as the excess of the carrying amount of goodwill (which would include the carrying amount of the acquired intangible asset) over the implied fair value of goodwill (which would exclude the fair value of the acquired intangible asset). (Paragraph 21 of Statement 141 requires that a portion of the fair value of the reporting unit be allocated to *all* of the assets of a reporting unit [including unrecognized intangible assets] in measuring the implied fair value of goodwill). For example, in Case B, a goodwill impairment loss would be measured by comparing the carrying amount of goodwill (which includes the carrying amount of the CDI asset) to the implied fair value of goodwill (which would *not* include the fair value of the CDI asset). Thus, a measured goodwill impairment loss might be larger than it would have been had an acquired intangible asset been recognized apart from goodwill.

November 14–15, 2001 EITF Meeting Minutes, p. 3   Administrative Matters

Exhibit 6.1   *(Continued)*

The FASB staff also notes that Statement 141 does not change the requirement to recognize an unidentifiable intangible asset pursuant to paragraph 5 of FASB Statement No. 72, *Accounting for Certain Acquisitions of Banking or Thrift Institutions.* The staff notes that Statement 72 applies to the acquisition of a commercial bank, a savings and loan association, a mutual savings bank, a credit union, other depository institutions having assets and liabilities of the same types as those institutions, and branches of such entities, regardless of whether the acquired entity or branch is considered to be "financially troubled." However, paragraph 5 of that Statement applies only to those acquisitions in which the fair value of the liabilities assumed by the acquiring entity exceeds the fair value of the tangible and recognized intangible assets acquired. Paragraph 5 requires that any excess of the fair value of the liabilities assumed over the fair value of the tangible and recognized intangible assets acquired be recognized as an unidentifiable intangible asset. For example, assume that on January 1, 20XI, a bank acquired a branch of another bank. The fair value of the liabilities assumed in that branch acquisition ($100) exceeds the fair value of the tangible and recognized intangible assets acquired ($80) by *$20.* Statement 141 does not change the requirement in Statement 72 to recognize that *$20* excess as an unidentifiable intangible asset. Moreover, Statement 142 does not change the requirement to amortize that intangible asset in accordance with the method prescribed in paragraph 5 of Statement 72.

Exhibit 6.2 FASB Staff Announcement—Topic No. D-101

Topic: Clarification of Reporting Unit Guidance in Paragraph 30 of FASB Statement No. 142

Date Discussed: November 14–15, 2001

An FASB representative announced that the staff has received inquiries about the application of paragraph 30 of FASB Statement No. 142, *Goodwill and Other Intangible Assets.* In particular, the inquiries have focused on the meaning of the phrase *discrete financial information.*

Paragraph 30 of Statement No. 142 includes the following guidance for determining reporting units:

> A reporting unit is an operating segment or one level below an operating segment (referred to as a component).[17] A component of an operating segment is a reporting unit if the component constitutes a business[18] for which discrete financial information is available and segment management[19] regularly reviews the operating results of that component. However, two or more components of an operating segment shall be aggregated and deemed a single reporting unit if the components have similar economic characteristics.[20] An operating segment shall be deemed to be a reporting unit if all of its components are similar, if none of its components is a reporting unit, or if it comprises only a single component. The relevant provisions of Statement 131 and related interpretative literature shall be used to determine the reports of an entity.

This staff announcement summarizes the FASB staff's understanding of the Board's intent with respect to the determination of whether a component of an operating segment is a reporting unit.

Determining whether a component of an operating segment is a reporting unit is a matter of judgment based on an entity's individual facts and circumstances. Although paragraph 30 of Statement 142 includes a number of characteristics that must be present for a component of an operating segment to be a reporting unit, no single factor or characteristic is determinative. The FASB staff believes that how an entity manages its operations and how an acquired entity is integrated with acquiring entity are key to determining the re-

[17] For purposes of determining reporting units, an operating segment is defined in paragraph 10 of FASB Statement No. 131, *Disclosures about Segments of an Enterprise and Related Information.*

[18] Emerging Issues Task Force Issue No. 98-3, "Determining Whether a Nonmonetary Transaction Involves Receipt of Productive Assets or of a Business," includes guidance on determining whether an asset group constitutes a business.

[19] Segment management consists of one or more segment managers, as that term is defined in paragraph 14 of Statement 131.

[20] Paragraph 17 of Statement 131 shall be considered in determining if the components of an operating segment have similar economic characteristics.

November 14–15, 2001 EITF Meeting Minutes, p. 1   Administrative Matters

Exhibit 6.2 *(Continued)*

porting units of the entity. As noted in the basis for conclusions of Statement 142, "The Board's intent was that a reporting unit would be the level of internal reporting that reflects the way an entity manages its business or operations and to which goodwill naturally would be associated" (paragraph B102). "That approach reflects the Board's belief that the information an entity reports for its internal use will reflect the way the overall entity is managed (paragraph B103)."

The characteristics identified in paragraph 30 of Statement 142 that must be present for a component to be a reporting unit are discussed below.

The Component Constitutes a Business
The determination of whether a component constitutes a business requires judgment based on specific facts and circumstances. The guidance in EITF Issue No. 98-3 "Determining Whether a Nonmonetary Transaction Involves Receipt of Productive Assets or of a Business," should be considered in determining whether a group of assets constitutes a business. That guidance states that, among other things, "for a transferred set of activities and assets to be a business, it must contain all of the inputs and processes necessary for it to continue to conduct normal operations after the transferred set is separated from the transferor." The fact that operating information (revenues and expenses) exists for a component of an operating segment does not mean that the component constitutes a business. For example, a component for which operating information is prepared might be a product line or a brand that is part of a business rather than a business itself.

Discrete Financial Information
The term *discrete financial information* should be applied in the same manner that it is applied in determining operating segments in accordance with paragraph 10 of Statement 131. The Statement 131 implementation guidance indicates that it is not necessary that assets be allocated for a component to be considered an operating segment (that is, no balance sheet is required). Thus, discrete financial information can constitute as little as operating information. Therefore, in order to test goodwill for impairment in accordance with Statement 142, an entity may be required to assign assets and liabilities to reporting units (consistent with the guidance in paragraphs 32 and 33 of Statement 142).

Reviewed by Segment Management
Segment management, as defined in paragraph 14 of Statement 131, is either a level below or the same level as the chief operating decision maker. According to Statement 131, a segment manager is "directly accountable to and maintains regular contact with the chief operating decision maker to discuss operating activities, financial results, forecasts, or plans for the segment." The approach used in Statement 142 to determine reporting units is similar to the one used to determine operating segments in Statement 131; however, Statement 142 focuses on how operating segments are managed rather than how the entity as a whole is managed. The approach in Statement 142 is consistent with the Board's intent that reporting units should reflect the way an entity manages its operations.

November 14–15, 2001 EITF Meeting Minutes, p. 2   Administrative Matters

Exhibit 6.2 *(Continued)*

Similar Economic Characteristics

Evaluating whether two components have similar economic characteristics is a matter of judgment that depends on specific facts and circumstances. That assessment should be more qualitative than quantitative.

In determining whether the components of an operating segment have similar economic characteristics, footnote 20 to paragraph 30 of Statement 142 states that the guidance in paragraph 17 of Statement 131 should be considered. The Board intended that all of the factors in paragraph 17 of Statement 131 be considered in making that determination. However, the Board did not intend that *every* factor must be met in order for two components to be considered economically similar. In addition the Board did not intend that the determination of whether two components economically similar be limited to consideration of the factors described in paragraph 17 of Statement 131. In determining whether components should be combined into one reporting unit based on their economic similarities, factors that should be considered in addition to those in paragraph 17 include but are not limited to:

- The manner in which an entity operates its business and the nature of those operations.
- Whether goodwill is recoverable from the separate operations of each component business or from two or more component businesses working in concert (which might be the case if the components are economically interdependent).
- The extent to which the component businesses share assets and other resources, as might be evidenced by extensive transfer pricing mechanisms.
- Whether the components support and benefit from common research and development projects.

The fact that a component extensively shares assets and other resources with other components of the operating segment may be an indication that the component either is not a business or may be economically similar to those other components.

Components that share similar economic characteristics but relate to different operating segments may not be combined into a single reporting unit. For example, an entity might have organized its operating segments on a geographic basis. If its three operating segments (Americas, Europe, and Asia) each have two components (A and B) that are dissimilar to each other but similar to the corresponding components in the other operating segments, the entity would *not* be permitted to combine component A from each of the operating segments to make reporting unit A.

Additional Observations

Some constituents have noted that two operating segments may have been aggregated into a reportable segment by applying the aggregation criteria in paragraph 17 of Statement 131, and have inquired about whether one or more of the components of those operating segments can be reporting units under Statement 142. The FASB staff believes it would be possible for one or more of those components to be economically dissimilar from the other components and thus be a reporting unit for the purposes of testing good-

Exhibit 6.2 *(Continued).*

will for impairment. In particular, the FASB staff believes that that situation might occur when an entity's operating segments are based on geographic areas. The following points need to be considered in addressing this question:

The determination of reporting units under Statement 142 begins with the definition of an operating segment in paragraph 10 of Statement 131 and considers *disaggregating* that operating segment into economically dissimilar components for the purpose of testing goodwill for impairment. The determination of reportable segments under Statement 131 also begins with a paragraph 10 operating segment, but considers whether certain economically similar operating segments should be *aggregated* into a single operating segment or a reportable segment.

- The level at which operating performance is reviewed differs between the two Statements—it is the chief operating decision maker who reviews operating segments and the segment manager who reviews reporting units (components of operating segments). Therefore, a component of an operating segment would not be considered an operating segment for Statement 131 purposes unless the chief operating decision maker regularly reviews its operating performance; however, that same component might be a reporting unit under Statement 142 if a segment manager regularly reviews its operating performance (and if other reporting unit criteria are met).

November 14–15, 2001 EITF Meeting Minutes, p. 4   Administrative Matters

Exhibit 6.3 FASB Proposal for a New Agenda Project

FINANCIAL ACCOUNTING STANDARDS BOARD

Proposal for a New Agenda Project

DISCLOSURE OF INFORMATION ABOUT INTANGIBLE ASSETS
NOT RECOGNIZED IN FINANCIAL STATEMENTS

This Proposal discusses a proposed FASB project to establish standards for improving disclosure of information about intangible assets that are not recognized in financial statements. This Proposal is part of an August 17, 2001 request for comments about the objective and scope of this project, as well as a proposed project on reporting financial performance.[1] Comments are requested by September 19, 2001.

DESCRIPTION OF THE PROPOSED PROJECT

This potential FASB *project on disclosure about intangibles* would focus on improving information about intangible assets that are seen by many as increasingly important to business success but are not currently recognized as assets in financial statements. Intangible assets are generally recognized only if acquired, either separately or as part of a business combination. Intangible assets that are generated internally, and some acquired assets that are written off immediately after being acquired, are not reflected in financial statements, and little quantitative or qualitative information about them is reported in the notes to the financial statements.

The principal goals of the project would be to make new information available to investors and creditors and to improve the quality of information currently being provided—information vital to well-reasoned investment and credit resource allocation decisions. A secondary goal of the project would be to take a first step in what might become an evolution toward recognition in an entity's financial statements of internally generated intangible assets.

The balance of this Proposal discusses the problem to be addressed, the scope of the project, the issues that would have to be resolved, how practice might change, and the FASB agenda criteria. It concludes with a request for comments and several questions for constituents.

---

[1] Further information about that request, including the Proposal for the project on reporting financial performance, is available at www.fasb.org/project/proposals.html.

© 2001. Financial Accounting Standards Board. Used with permission.

Exhibit 6.3   *(Continued)*

THE PROBLEM

Hundreds of recent articles, studies, and consultants' reports have decried what they consider accounting's failures to respond to recent fundamental changes in the economy. Some suggest that the important value drivers in the new economy are largely nonfinancial, and that a set of measures could and should be developed that would allow investors and creditors to better evaluate entities and compare them with one another. Others suggest that the importance of intangibles is the distinguishing feature of the new economy, that intangible assets are recognized in financial statements only when acquired from others, and that accounting standard setters should require information about internally generated intangible assets. This proposed project would respond to those suggestions.

One aspect of the problem is comparability. Intangible assets are generally recognized in financial statements if they are acquired, either by themselves or as part of a business combination. However, otherwise identical intangible assets generally are not recognized if developed internally. It is therefore difficult to compare the financial statements of an entity that has built up substantial intangible assets internally with those of another entity that has purchased most of its intangible assets. Disclosure can help diligent investors in making such a comparison, but quantitative disclosures are currently required only about the recognized intangible assets.[2] Therefore, the comparative procedure available now is to subtract all recognized intangibles, which allows investors to compare adjusted amounts that ignore all intangible assets. In view of the increasing importance of intangibles, that approach is suboptimal. Disclosures about unrecognized intangibles would potentially allow investors to make a more complete comparison.

Without the leadership of the FASB, the IASB, or other standard-setting or regulatory bodies, it is unlikely that companies will consistently provide financial statement users with reasonably comparable information about intangible assets. Users of financial reports will continue to find relatively little information in the financial statements about key value drivers, and to have little confidence in what information they do receive.

---

[2] FASB Statement No. 142, *Goodwill and Other Intangible Assets*, issued in June 2001, improves disclosures about recognized intangible assets and about research and development assets in the year they are written off immediately after being acquired, but it does not address unrecognized intangibles.

© 2001. Financial Accounting Standards Board. Used with permission.

Exhibit 6.3 *(Continued)*

THE SCOPE

The principal source material for this Proposal is the April 2001 Special Report, *Business and Financial Reporting, Challenges from the New Economy*, by former FASB staff member Wayne S. Upton Jr. (the New Economy Report), which is available on the FASB website (www.fasb.org/new_economy.html) or in print from the FASB order department. The New Economy Report suggested four possible FASB projects. This potential FASB project on disclosure about intangibles would take on one of those suggestions, to address the format and content of disclosure about unrecognized intangible assets. That might be a first step in an evolution toward recognition of some internally generated intangible assets, or the disclosure project might be undertaken without any presumption about eventual recognition. Either way, it would stimulate companies to identify intangible assets and other value drivers and to collect some information about intangibles not previously captured in management reporting systems. It would also allow standard setters to refine the definition of an intangible asset and, most importantly, would provide investors, creditors, and other users of financial reports with additional information to assess an entity's intangible assets.

This Proposal suggests a project scope focused on disclosure about intangible assets that are not recognized in statements of financial position, but would have been recognized if acquired either separately or in a business combination. It would also include in-process research and development assets that, under FASB Interpretation No. 4, *Applicability of FASB Statement No. 2 to Business Combinations Accounted for by the Purchase Method*, are written off to expense on the day they are acquired.

Other project scopes have been suggested. One would be *disclosure of nonfinancial indicators* about intangible factors, such as market size and share, customer satisfaction levels, new product success rates, and employee retention rates. Another would be *recognition and measurement*, in statements of financial position, *of research and development and other project-related intangible assets*. A third would be *separate recognition and measurement of intangible assets or liabilities embedded* in tangible or financial assets, for example, banks' core deposit intangibles and insurers' claim-handling obligations.[3] The Board does not propose to include those matters in this potential project but welcomes comments from constituents on that conclusion.

---

[3] The New Economy Report identified that possible project on recognition of embedded intangibles and service obligations. The proposed project on disclosure about intangibles would not touch on those issues, many of which are closely related to and may be inseparable from issues under active consideration in the Board's project on measuring financial assets and liabilities at fair value.

Exhibit 6.3 *(Continued)*

RELEVANT RESEARCH, ISSUES, AND CONCERNS

The project would include considering matters raised in, and comments received by the FASB and other standard-setting bodies on the recommendations of the:

1. November 1993 report of the Association for Investment Management and Research (AIMR), *Financial Reporting in the 1990s and Beyond*

2. December 1994 report of the American Institute of Certified Public Accountants (AICPA) Special Committee on Financial Reporting, *Improving Business Reporting— A Customer Focus*

3. January 2001 report of the Business Reporting Research Project, *Improving Business Reporting: Insights into Enhancing Voluntary Disclosures*

The substantial body of research by Professor Baruch Lev of New York University and others summarized in the New Economy Report also should be of considerable assistance in resolving the principal issues in this project.

The initial phase of the project would build on those and other earlier efforts. A first step would be to establish a working group of outside experts to assist the FASB, especially in identifying the relevant issues and possible solutions and in refining user surveys.

After Board deliberations, an Exposure Draft, and consideration of comments from constituents, the project would result in a final Statement calling for disclosures. The project is expected to take about two years.

The Principal Issues

The first issue, alluded to in the discussion of scope, is *what intangible assets are to be covered* by the Statement. The proposed scope is intangible assets that are not recognized, but would have been recognized had they been acquired from others, as well as in-process research and development assets written off after acquisition. The project would consider whether existing guidance[4] is adequate for preparers and practitioners to determine what is and is not included, or whether additional guidance is needed. The conceptual analysis in Chapter 4 of the New Economy Report should be useful in resolving that scope issue.[5]

---

[4] For example, in FASB Statements No. 141, *Business Combinations*, and No. 142, *Goodwill and Other Intangible Assets*.

[5] Part 2 of Chapter 4 of the New Economy Report presents a list of intangible assets, classified according to whether they are separable from the entity and whether they are based on contractual or other legal rights. The list includes agreements with suppliers and customers, rights to scarce resources, permits, franchises, patents and copyrights, computer programs, secret formulas and processes, databases, and research and development, among others.

© 2001. Financial Accounting Standards Board. Used with permission.

Exhibit 6.3 *(Continued)*

The second principal issue is *what information should be disclosed* about intangible assets. Possible quantitative and qualitative disclosures about unrecognized intangible assets might include:

- Major classes of intangible assets and their characteristics

- Expenditures to develop and maintain them

- Values of those assets[6]

- Significant events that change the anticipated future benefits arising from intangible assets.

The *time gap* and the *correlation gap* between expenditures and values of resulting intangible assets, noted on page ix of the New Economy Report, will present challenges in resolving what information should be disclosed.

The FASB conceptual framework contains only general guidance about disclosure, mainly focused on qualitative characteristics, which will be of limited help to the Board in selecting from the alternatives those that will best improve financial reporting. A second concern is that it may not be feasible to develop and verify some of the information about intangibles that is desired by some investors, creditors, and other users of financial reports.

Other Issues

Should the Disclosures Be Voluntary or Required?

The Business Reporting Steering Committee and others suggest that, in view of such factors as the variations between and even within industries, disclosures should be voluntary. That would certainly reduce resistance to the proposed Statement. However, the potential participation level in response to encouraging voluntary disclosures may not be acceptable.[7]

Should the Disclosures Be Made Annually or More Frequently?

Most FASB requirements for disclosure effectively apply only to the full sets of financial statements and notes commonly presented in annual financial reports. Some information is required to be disclosed in interim financial information, and the Board could require that for information about intangibles.

---

[6] While the main emphasis of this project would be on unrecognized intangible assets, the project might also consider disclosures about values of recognized intangible assets.

[7] For example, FASB Statement 119, *Disclosure about Derivative Financial Instruments and Fair Value [of] Financial Instruments*, encouraged disclosure of quantitative information about market risks of derivative instruments in 1994, but few entities reported such information until the SEC mandated it in 1997. FASB Statement No. 89, *Financial Reporting and Changing Prices*, encouraged continued disclosure of current-cost and constant-purchasing-power information, but very few entities provide it.

Exhibit 6.3   *(Continued)*

Concerns Likely to Be Raised

Users of financial reports will likely support improvements in information about unrecognized intangibles. On the other hand, preparers of financial reports and their auditors may have concerns regarding competitive harm, fears of failure to meet expectations, lack of expertise, and preparations costs.

However, not taking on such a project may mean that financial reports continue to fall to provide information about what many argue are increasingly the main drivers of values in the capital markets. Chapter 1 of the New Economy Report discusses those arguments.

AGENDA CRITERIA

This Proposal is one of several means by which the Board seeks to obtain advice from its constituents about possible additions to its technical agenda. After receiving input from constituents, the Board must make its own decisions regarding its technical agenda. To aid in the decision-making process, the Board has developed a list of factors to which it refers in evaluating proposed topics. Those factors, which are more fully discussed in *Facts about FASB* include consideration of (a) the pervasiveness of the issue, (b) alternative solutions, (c) technical feasibility, and (d) practical consequences. At this time, the Board believes that this proposed project on disclosures about intangibles satisfies each of those factors. However, the Board's resources are limited and it is aware of other potential projects suggested by constituents that also satisfy those factors.

In addition, the Board has determined that all topics under consideration for the FASB's agenda should be assessed to determine whether they provide opportunities for cooperative efforts with the IASB or other national standard setters. More specifically, that assessment is to include consideration of (a) the possibility that resolution of the issues addressed would increase convergence of standards worldwide, (b) the opportunities the topic presents for cooperation with the IASB or other standard setters, and (c) whether appropriate and sufficient resources are available for a joint project or other cooperative effort. In contrast to some other proposed projects, it seems less likely, given their other priorities and resource constraints, that the IASB or other national standard setters will address information about intangibles in the near term. Therefore, the FASB would likely be working separately on this proposed project. However, the same concerns that have been noted in the United States will likely be heard in other countries.

Exhibit 6.3 *(Continued)*

REQUEST FOR COMMENTS

The Board has not decided whether to add a project on reporting information about intangibles to its agenda or about the scope of such a project. The Board is seeking comments from its constituents on this Proposal, particularly on the following major questions:

1. Is there a need for the FASB or others to comprehensively address the reporting of information about intangibles of a business enterprise? If yes, should the FASB take on such an effort or defer to others? If so, to whom?

2. Is the proposed scope of such a project as described in this Proposal insufficient, appropriate, or too ambitious? One alternative would be a broader scope that might encompass other constituent recommendations, for example, (a) disclosure about nonfinancial indicators, management's key goals for them, and related risks, strategies, efforts, and accomplishments in meeting its goals or (b) recognition and measurement of certain internally generated intangible assets. Another alternative would be a limited-scope project that focuses solely on, for example, disclosure of expenditures to develop and maintain unrecognized intangible assets or on disclosure of information about research and development activities.

3. Should specific issues identified above be excluded from the scope of the proposed project on reporting information about intangibles? If yes, for each specific issue, please indicate whether it should be addressed as part of another FASB project, by others, or not at all and why.

4. Should specific issues not identified above be addressed as part of the proposed project on reporting information about intangibles? If yes, please describe the specific issue and indicate why it is sufficiently crucial that it should be addressed as part of the proposed project.

Chapter 7

Implementation Aids

The Securities and Exchange Commission is concerned that financial statements properly reflect acquired assets at their fair values. It is safe to assume that they will place a similar level of emphasis on nonamortizable assets as they have on in-process research and development, and will be looking for instances of overvaluation of nonamortizable intangible assets. Management should be aware that the overvaluation of nonamortizable assets increases the potential of later having to recognize impairment charges on such assets. If impairment losses become commonplace, investors may begin to question management's ability to make successful acquisitions. Therefore, it is vital that purchase price allocations and impairment testing be done by a qualified professional.

Management may conduct impairment testing internally *only if company personnel can meet the criteria of Statement on Auditing Standards (SAS) 73, Using the Work of a Specialist.* Auditors will be reviewing management's qualifications and work product to ensure that the requirements of SAS 73 and SFAS Nos. 141 and 142 are met. Most auditors are interpreting the new independence standards as not allowing the auditor to perform SFAS Nos. 141 and 142 services.

The services of an independent valuation specialist are usually required in estimating the fair value of assets acquired in a business combination. Some entities employ valuation specialists in their organizations; others will find it necessary to engage the services of an external valuation specialist. Regardless of who performs the valuation, the auditor should determine that the specialist has the requisite skills and expertise to develop a valuation of the acquired assets in conformity with generally accepted accounting principles.

A review of the qualifications of the appraiser should be at the same high level of any critical professional. These qualifications should focus on the appraiser's skill, education, and experience and may include:

- Specialized training in business valuation
- Specialized training in valuing intangible assets
- Audit experience or exposure to comprehend the audit environment for the valuation
- Recognized business valuation designations
- Postgraduate education
- Professional leadership activities at the state or national level
- Unique professional activity such as serving on task forces or committees for organizations like the SEC, FASB, or AICPA on these issues
- Knowledge of the elements of SFAS Nos. 141 and 142 including critically related SFAS as 121 (impairment) and 131 (segment reporting) as well as others
- Experience in rendering opinions related to intangible assets
- Experience defending valuation opinions (e.g., SEC)

So, what steps should companies take when faced with implementing SFAS Nos. 141 and 142? We recommend that the company:

- Consider creating new accounts to capture adjustments that may be needed to effectively provide the information necessary for goodwill impairment testing
- Clarify management's role in data gathering
- Get the auditors involved as soon as possible
- Select appraisers and involve them as soon as possible
- Clearly define the scope of the engagement and the responsibilities and expectations of each of the involved parties (company management, auditors, and appraisers)
- Promptly complete financial statements before the due dates

The steps outlined in *Procedures for the Valuation of Intangible Assets* (Exhibit 7.1 at the end of the chapter), are provided to assist auditors, management, and valuation analysts in compiling operational information that will aid in assigning values to intangible assets acquired in a business combination. These procedures will also assist in determining the appropriate valuation approach for each intangible asset (i.e., cost, market, income). The *Intangible Asset Data Request* (Exhibit 7.2 at the end of the chapter) should be used with the above procedures to assist in gathering necessary information.

A portion of the purchase price in a purchase business combination may be allocated to in-process research and development (IPR&D), but IPR&D is particularly common in acquisitions of software, electronic devices, and pharmaceutical companies. The *Model Audit Program* (Exhibit 7.3) outlines audit procedures that should be considered when an entity has consummated a purchase business combination that may involve IPR&D.

The *Model Audit Program* procedures focus on the software, electronic devices, and pharmaceutical industries. Further tailoring of the recommended procedures may be necessary upon review of the specific circumstances of each acquisition. These modifications may be influenced by the business, legal, and regulatory environments of both the acquiring company and the acquiree. Hence, in tailoring the recommended procedures to each acquisition, the auditors should apply their professional judgment in correlation with the knowledge of the environments of the acquiring company and the acquiree.

Exhibit 7.1   Procedures for the Valuation of Intangible Assets

---

BUSINESS NAME: _____

VALUATION DATE: _____

The definition of intangible asset should include current and non-current assets (excluding financial instruments) that lack physical substance. An intangible asset acquired in a business combination shall be recognized as an asset apart from goodwill if that asset arises from contractual or other legal rights. If an intangible asset does not arise from contractual or other legal rights, it shall be recognized as an asset apart from goodwill only if it is separable; that is, if it is capable of being separated or divided from the acquired enterprise and sold, transferred, licensed, rented, or exchanged (regardless of whether there is an intent to do so). For GAAP purposes, an intangible asset that cannot be sold, transferred, licensed, rented, or exchanged individually is considered separable if it can be sold, transferred, licensed, rented, or exchanged with a related contract, asset, or liability. However, the value of an assembled workforce of at-will employees acquired in a business combination shall be included in the amount recorded as goodwill regardless of whether it meets the criteria for recognition apart from goodwill.

Please complete the following to the best of your ability:

1. Determine the standard of value:
   a. Fair market value
   b. Fair value
   c. Investment value
   d. Intrinsic value or fundamental value
   e. _____

2. State the purpose of the valuation:
   _____

3. Determine the premise of value:
   a. Value in use, as part of a going concern (This premise contemplates the contributory value to an income-producing enterprise of the intangible asset as part of a mass assemblage of tangible and intangible assets.)
   b. Value in place, as part of an assemblage of assets (This premise contemplates that the intangible asset is fully functional, is part of an assemblage of assets that is ready for use but is not currently engaged in the production of income.)
   c. Value in exchange, in an orderly disposition (This premise contemplates that the intangible asset will be sold in its current condition, with normal exposure to its appropriate secondary market, but without the contributory value of any associated tangible or intangible assets.)
   d. Value in exchange, in a forced liquidation (This premise contemplates that the intangible asset is sold piecemeal, in an auction environment, with an artificially abbreviated exposure to its secondary market.)

Exhibit 7.1 *(Continued)*

4. Is the intangible asset subject to specific identification and recognizable description

5. Categorize the intangible asset as:
   a. Marketing related
   b. Customer related
   c. Artistic related
   d. Contract related
   e. Technology related

6. Determine the intangible assets eligible for appraisal.

   List:

   _____

   _____

   _____

   _____

7. Describe fully the intangible asset identified. Attach necessary contracts, drawings, patents, listings, and so on to fully identify the intangible asset.

8. Describe the legal existence and protection associated with the intangible asset.

9. Is the transferability of the ownership restricted? Explain.

10. Describe the susceptibility of the asset being destroyed.

11. Describe the inception of the intangible asset (attach a list providing start dates for all customer or client lists).

12. To what degree is the revenue associated with these intangible assets due to the day-to-day efforts of the owner? Explain.

13. Provide isolated financial results directly related to the asset, such as:
    • Historical cost to create the asset
    • Annual cost to maintain the asset
    • Specific cash flow related to the asset

14. Provide a description of the history of the asset, including year(s) created.

15. Provide all contracts or agreements.

16. Provide all strategic, marketing, and business plans related to the asset.

17. Provide all market or industry surveys or studies related to the asset.

Exhibit 7.1   *(Continued)*

18. Describe the competitive environment related to the asset.

19. Describe the general economic environment related to the asset.

20. Describe the specific industry environment related to the asset.

21. Provide all previous valuation reports related to the asset.

22. Provide all financial projections including unit sales.

23. Provide all budgets/forecasts.

24. Determine associated cost of capital related directly to the asset.

25. At what stage in its life cycle is the asset?

26. Describe the product life cycle.

27. Determine valuation approach:
    a. Cost approach
    b. Market approach
    c. Income approach

COST APPROACH

The cost approach is based on the principle of substitution. A prudent investor would not pay more for an intangible asset than it would cost to replace that intangible asset with a ready-made comparable substitute. Some intangible assets likely to be valued using the cost approach include computer software, automated databases, technical drawings and documentation, blueprints and engineering drawings, laboratory notebooks, technical libraries, chemical formulations, food and other product recipes, and so on.

28. Determine the appropriate cost method.
    a. Reproduction cost (The cost at current prices to construct an exact duplicate or replica of the subject intangible asset. This duplicate would be created using the same materials, standards, design, layout, and quality of workmanship used to create the original intangible asset.)
    b. Replacement cost (The cost to create at current prices an asset having equal utility to the intangible asset. Replacement cost utilizes modern methods and standards, state of the art design and layout and the highest available quality of workmanship.)

29. Determine the appropriate adjustment for obsolescence.
    a. Physical deterioration (The reduction from cost due to physical wear and tear resulting from continued use.)
    b. Functional obsolescence (The reduction due to the inability to perform the function or yield the periodic utility for which the asset was originally designed.)
    c. Technological obsolescence (The reduction due to improvements in technology that make an asset less than an ideal replacement for itself, generally resulting in improvements in design or engineering technology and resulting in greater standardized measure of utility production.)
    d. Economic obsolescence (The reduction due to the effects, events, or conditions that are not controlled by, and thus external to, the current use or condition of the subject asset.)

© 2002. The Financial Valuation Group, LC. Used with permission.

Exhibit 7.1 *(Continued)*

30. Determine the number of employees involved in creating the intangible asset.

31. Categorize the employees by salary level.

32. Capture the associated employer cost related to each hour of salary level.

33. Determine the number of hours per employee salary level utilized to develop the asset.

34. Extend the number of hours per salary level by the salary and associated employer cost for an estimate of reproduction costs new.

35. Adjust reproduction cost new for associated deterioration or obsolescence.

36. Compare net result of reproduction cost with replacement cost new.

37. Complete the cost approach analysis.

MARKET APPROACH

The market approach compares the subject intangible asset with similar or comparable intangible assets that have been sold or listed for sale in the appropriate primary or secondary market. Correlations must be extrapolated.

38. Determine the market served by the guideline or comparable asset.

39. Complete a primary and secondary market search for similar guideline assets, including an analysis of available public data specific to royalty rates and intellectual property transactions.

40. Determine the historical return on the investment earned by the subject intangible asset.

41. Determine the income generating capacity of the subject intangible asset.

42. Determine the expected prospective return on the investment earned by the guideline asset.

43. Determine the expected prospective return by the subject intangible asset.

44. Determine the historical age and expected remaining useful life of the guideline or comparable intangible asset.

45. Determine the historical age and the remaining useful life of the subject intangible asset.

46. Analyze the terms of the sale of the guideline or the comparable intangible asset including:
    - The time of the sale
    - The price paid
    - The payout terms
    - Other related terms (including special seller financing and earn-out agreement, non-compete agreement, and so on)

Exhibit 7.1   *(Continued)*

47. Determine the degree of adjustment necessary to the guideline or comparable intangible asset related to:
    a. Physical deterioration
    b. Functional obsolescence
    c. Technological obsolescence
    d. Economic obsolescence

48. Determine the degree of adjustment necessary to the subject intangible asset related to:
    a. Physical deterioration
    b. Functional obsolescence
    c. Technological obsolescence
    d. Economic obsolescence

49. Complete extrapolation of market approach correlation.

INCOME APPROACH

50. Determine the economic income related to the identified intangible asset for the following:
    a. Net income before tax
    b. Net income after tax
    c. Net operating income
    d. Gross rental income
    e. Gross royalty or license income (actual or hypothetical if a relief from royalties method is employed, in which case should include an analysis of available public data specific to royalty rates and intellectual property transactions)
    f. Gross or operating cash flow
    g. Net or free cash flow

51. Determine the direct cost associated with maintaining the identified intangible asset. These costs should include cost of operating the asset, storing the asset (facilities), and managing a return from the asset (staff expenses). Pay particular attention to any anticipated unusual costs (such as renewing a patent).

52. Determine specific cash flow to the intangible asset by taking an economic return on contributory assets that are part of the initial cash flow stream. Contributory assets include:
    • Working capital
    • Fixed assets
    • Other intangible assets

© 2002. The Financial Valuation Group, LC. Used with permission.

Exhibit 7.1 *(Continued)*

53. Determine an appropriate discount rate reflecting a fair return on the investment by considering:

    a. The opportunity cost of capital

    b. The term period of the investment (including consideration of the expected remaining life of the subject intangible asset)

    c. The systematic risk of the investment

    d. The unsystematic risk of the investment

    e. The time value of money

    f. Growth (utilized for computing terminal value)

54. Obtain the necessary data to complete the actuarial retirement rate methodology including:

    • Inception dates for all active files

    • Inception dates and retirement dates for all inactive files comprising the subject intangible asset (5-year history desirable)

55. In absence of hard data for No. 54 above, obtain management's representations as to:

    • Average age of all active files

    • Average remaining life of all active files

    • "Estimate the number of visits per file"

56. Complete the actuarial retirement rate methodology by:

    • Observing the data

    • Determine the curve fitting using appropriate statistical tools

        • S-curve

        • O-curve

        • L-curve

        • R-curve

57. Match the actuarial retirement rate curve with the actual data.

58. Determine the probable life curve.

59. Determine the remaining useful life and survivorship percentages.

60. Apply the survivorship percentages to the discounted cash flow.

61. Complete income approach methodology.

RELIEF FROM ROYALTIES METHOD

62. How is the licensed product unique? What are the competitive advantages of the licensed product including the scope and remaining life of any patents related to the products?

Exhibit 7.1 *(Continued)*

63. Analyze the markets in which the licensee will sell the licensed products, including:

    a. Market size

    b. Growth rates

    c. Extent of competition

    d. Recent developments

64. Determine the degree of complexity in the sale of the licensed product.

65. Determine the extent of customization in customer-specific applications. (Note: Royalty rates are generally inversely related to the level of complexity and licensee customization.)

66. Determine the size of the licensed territory, including any restrictions or exclusivity. (Note: Exclusivity is directly correlated to higher royalty rates.)

67. Determine the length of the initial license term and provisions for renewal. (Note: Royalty rates will increase if the provisions for renewal are favorable for licensing.)

68. What are the provisions for termination? (Note: The conditions for unilateral license termination generally protect the licensor from a material breach committed by the licensee. These terms should be identified.)

69. Does a minimum royalty rate exist?

70. Analyze the licensee's ability to assign the license to a third party, either directly or indirectly (for instance through the purchase of stock ownership).

71. What is the licensor's presence within its own markets?

72. What is the licensor's financial viability?

73. What is the licensor's size and market share?

74. What is the licensor's depth of senior management and stability?

75. What is the licensor's depth of technical knowledge?

76. What is the licensor's business plan related to the licensed products, including R&D funding and market analysis?

77. To what extent and timeliness does the licensor offer to support the licensee including:

    a. Technical product advice

    b. Assisting the licensee with sales

    c. Assisting the licensee with marketing efforts in the defined territory

Exhibit 7.1 *(Continued)*

78. Determine the licensee's available profit percentage available for the royalty (25%?, 50%?) dependent upon the following:

    a. Available profitability as compared with the industry

    b. The nature of the long-term competitive advantage of the product

    c. The degree the license terms are favorable to the licensee

    d. The degree of support and market share offered by the licensor

    e. The degree of any noncash value offered by the licensee to the licensor

    f. The degree the licensee is required to purchase certain components used in the manufacturing of licensed products from the licensor (mandatory supply arrangement)

    g. The degree of foreign exchange risk borne by either the licensee or the licensor (the risk of future devaluation).

Exhibit 7.2 Intangible Asset Data Request

BUSINESS NAME:_____

VALUATION DATE:_____

This is a generalized information request. Some items may not pertain to your company, and some items may not be readily available to you. In such cases, please indicate N/A or notify us if other arrangements can be made to obtain the data. Items already provided have been marked with an "X." If you have any questions on the development of this information, please call.

A. Patents

____ 1. Provide a summary of patents held by the Company.

____ 2. Provide copies of patent applications and patent abstracts.

____ 3. Distinguish which patents have commercial applications (i.e., are producing or are reasonably forecast to produce revenue in the future).

____ 4. Provide historical cost records documenting development of the patent(s):
   a. Person hours to develop
   b. Various technical levels of persons working on the assignment
   c. Pay scales for individuals in 4b
   d. Information to determine overhead rate

____ 5. Identify patents and associated products that now have or are expected to have commercial viability.
   a. Prepare forecast or projection of revenues related to patent over the life of the patent
   b. Project direct expenses associated with producing revenue in 5a

____ 6. Comment on the possibility of extending patent protection beyond statutory life of patent.

____ 7. Provide details of any patents you are licensing in or out.

B. Copyrights

____ 8. Provide a list of all copyrighted registrations.

____ 9. Provide a list of works (articles, books, painting, etc.).

10. Identify copyright names that are associated with products and/or services (such as software or report templates).

11. Identify historical sale of products and/or services employing the works for the last five years.

12. Provide projection of products and/or services that will employ the works for the next five years.

13. Provide details of any copyrighted works you are licensing in or out.

Exhibit 7.2 *(Continued)*

___

C. Trademarks and Trade Names

____ 14. Provide a list of all trademark/trade name registrations.

____ 15. Provide a list of trademark/trade names that are not registered.

____ 16. Identify trademarks/trade names that are associated with products and/or services.

____ 17. Identify historical sale of products and/or services employing trademarks/trade names for the last five years.

____ 18. Provide projection of products and/or services that employ the trademarks/trade names for the next five years.

____ 19. Provide details of any trademarks/trade names you are licensing in or out.

D. Proprietary Processes/Products Technology

____ 20. Describe the proprietary process/product technology.

____ 21. Describe competitive advantages and disadvantages of the proprietary process/product technology.

____ 22. Describe industry trends and competitive pressures that may affect the useful life of the proprietary process/product technology.

____ 23. In light of 21 and 22 above, estimate the useful life of the proprietary process/product technology support.

____ 24. Describe products or services that employ the proprietary process/product technology.

____ 25. If available, provide historical cost records documenting development of the process/product technology:

   a. Person hours to develop

   b. Various technical levels of persons working on the assignment

   c. Pay scales for individuals in 25b

   d. Information to determine overhead rate

____ 26. In the absence of historical cost records, estimate effort to recreate the process/product technology if it were to be developed from scratch:

   a. Who would work on the assignment (employees and consultants)

   b. Pay rates for individuals in 26a

   c. Information to determine overhead rate

____ 27. Identify historical sale of products and/or services employing process/product technology for the last five years.

____ 28. Provide projection of products and/or services that employ the process/product technology for the next five years.

____ 29. Project revenues including licensing income for the lifespan of process/product technology.

Exhibit 7.2 *(Continued)*

_____ 30. Project direct expenses associated with producing revenue in 29.
_____ 31. Obtain or develop indirect expenses (i.e., overhead).
_____ 32. Provide details of any technology you are licensing in or out.

E.   Know-How

_____ 33. Describe know-how, including competitive advantages and disadvantages.
_____ 34. Describe industry trends and competitive pressures that may affect the useful life of the know-how.
_____ 35. In light of 33 and 34 above, estimate the useful life of the know-how.
_____ 36. List products or services that employ the know-how.
_____ 37. If available, provide historical cost records documenting development of the know-how:
     a. Person hours to develop
     b. Various technical levels of persons working on the assignment
     c. Pay scales for individuals in 37b
     d. Information to determine overhead rate
_____ 38. In the absence of historical cost records, estimate corporate effort to recreate the know-how if it were to be developed from scratch:
     a. Who would work on the assignment (employees and consultants)
     b. Pay rates for individuals in 38a
     c. Information to determine overhead rate
    39. Identify historical sale of revenues for products and/or services employing know-how for the last five years.
_____ 40. Know-how associated with products and/or services:
     a. Provide projection of products and/or services that employ the know-how for the next five years
     b. Project direct expenses associated with producing revenue in 40a
     c. Obtain or develop indirect expenses (i.e., overhead)
_____ 41. Provide details of any know-how you are licensing in or out.

F.   Software

_____ 42. Describe the function of the software.
_____ 43. For cost approach:
     a. If available, provide historical cost records documenting development of the software:
       (1) Person hours to develop
       (2) Various technical levels of persons working on the assignment
       (3) Pay scales for individuals in 43a(2)
       (4) Information to determine overhead rate
     b. In the absence of historical cost records, estimate effort to recreate the software if it were to be developed from scratch:
       (1) Who would work on the assignment (employees and consultants)

Exhibit 7.2 *(Continued)*

(2) Pay rates for individuals in 43b(1)

(3) Information to determine overhead rate

____ 44. Lifing/obsolescence:

a. Expected useful life at inception and at valuation date. Obtain support for estimate

b. Date software actually placed in use

c. Describe internal development that may extend life

d. Describe internal development of replacement software that might shorten life

e. Describe external factors that may affect life

____ 45. For income approach:

a. Obtain historical revenues applicable to software

b. Project revenues including licensing income for lifespan of software

c. Project direct expenses associated with producing revenue in 45b

d. Obtain or develop indirect expenses (i.e., overhead)

e. Identify expenses, direct and indirect, not associated with acquired software

G. Customer Relationships

____ 46. Provide customer sales history for the last five years for the top ten customers.

____ 47. Provide complete customer history for the last five years (this would be for lifing).

____ 48. Provide financial data representing annual costs for the last five years associated with developing/soliciting new customers.

____ 49. Provide schedule of new customers gained in each of the last five years with sales.

____ 50. For the last five years, number of customers in a given year that failed to purchase in the following year. Provide those customers' sales for the prior year.

H. General Information

____ 51. Financial statements for fiscal years ending FIVE YEARS.

____ 52. Interim financial statements for the year-to-date DATE OF VALUATION AND ONE YEAR PRIOR.

____ 53. Financial projections, if any, for the current year and the next three years. Include any prepared budgets and/or business plans.

____ 54. Federal and State Corporate Income Tax Returns and supporting schedules for fiscal years ending FIVE YEARS.

____ 55. Explanation of significant non-recurring and/or non-operating items appearing on the financial statements in any fiscal year if not detailed in footnotes.

____ 56. Provide copies of any appraisals of the stock of the Company made during the last three years.

____ 57. Provide copies of any appraisals of real estate or personal property owned by the Company.

Exhibit 7.2 *(Continued)*

_____ 58. Provide a summary of major covenants or agreements binding on the Company, e.g., union contracts, capital leases, employment contracts, service contracts, product warranties, etc.

_____ 59. List all subsidiary companies and the percentage ownership in each.

_____ 60. Name any "related" companies (common ownership, common shareholders, etc.) and briefly describe the relationship(s).

_____ 61. Provide all closing statements and purchase agreements related to all purchases of the Company's stock over the history of the Company.

_____ 62. Provide all closing statements and purchase agreements related to all mergers or acquisitions by the Company up to the valuation date.

_____ 63. Provide terms of any offers to purchase the Company.

Exhibit 7.3   Model Audit Program

General

A portion of the purchase price in a purchase business combination may be allocated to In-Process Research and Development (IPR&D), but IPR&D is particularly common in acquisitions of software, electronic devices, and pharmaceutical companies. This model audit program outlines audit procedures that should be considered when an entity has consummated a purchase business combination that may involve IPR&D.

The procedures focus on the software, electronic devices, and pharmaceutical industries; however, further tailoring of the recommended procedures may be necessary in response to the specific circumstances of each acquisition. The nature and extent of the needed tailoring may be influenced by the business, legal, and regulatory environments in which both the acquiring company and the acquiree operate. Accordingly, auditors should use their knowledge of those environments and their professional judgment in tailoring the recommended procedures to each acquisition.

The services of a valuation specialist are usually required in estimating the amount of the purchase price allocated to IPR&D. Some entities employ valuation specialists in their organizations; others will find it necessary to engage the services of an external valuation specialist. Regardless of who performs the valuation, the auditor should determine that the specialist has the requisite skills and expertise to develop a valuation of the acquired IPR&D in conformity with generally accepted accounting principles. In gathering audit evidence as to the appropriateness of the IPR&D valuation, the auditor may also require the assistance of a valuation specialist. That specialist may be an employee of the auditor's firm or may be an external valuation specialist engaged by the auditor to assist in evaluating the reasonableness of the IPR&D valuation.

Procedures

1. Obtain an understanding of the acquisition.

    a. Inquire of appropriate client personnel as to the nature and business purpose of the acquisition and whether special terms or conditions may exist.

        [*Persons of whom inquiry might be made include the CEO, the CFO, and appropriate personnel from marketing, business development, research and development, and technology departments. The auditor should become familiar with the types of products and services sold by the acquiree, and its production, marketing, distribution, and compensation methods. The auditor should also become aware of significant matters and trends affecting the industry, including economic conditions, changes in technology, government regulations, and competition.*]

    b. Obtain and read the acquisition agreements, due diligence reports prepared by client personnel or other parties engaged by the client, analyst's reports, acquiree prospectuses or offering memoranda, and other industry analyses pertinent to the acquisition.

    c. Obtain and read presentations to the board of directors and any press releases concerning the acquisition.

Exhibit 7.3 *(Continued)*

2. Ascertain the identity and affiliation of the valuation specialist. Arrange to meet with the valuation specialist and discuss the following:
    a. The objectives and scope of the valuation study.
    b. Whether the valuation specialist has any relationships with the client that might impair the valuation specialist's objectivity.
    c. The valuation specialist's understanding of the requirements of GAAP as they relate to the valuation.
    d. The types and sources of information to be provided by the acquiring company to the valuation specialist.
    e. The methods and significant assumptions used in the valuation.
    f. The consistency of methods and assumptions with previous valuations.
    g. The scope and nature of the conclusions included in the valuation report.
3. Ascertain the following:
    a. The professional competence of the valuation specialist as evidenced by accreditation or certification, licensure or recognition by a recognized professional organization.
    b. The professional reputation of the valuation specialist as viewed by his or her peers and others familiar with his or her capabilities or performance.
    c. The experience of the valuation specialist in the industry or in the valuation of tangible and intangible assets, including acquired IPR&D.
4. Inquire of client personnel regarding any relationship between the valuation specialist and the client.
    [The auditor should evaluate any relationship between the valuation specialist and the client to ascertain whether the client has the ability—through employment, ownership, contractual rights, family relationship, or otherwise—to directly or indirectly control or significantly influence the valuation specialist's work. The valuation report should identify such relationships.]
5. With respect to the valuation report:
    a. Determine whether the valuation methodology used reconciles to the AICPA Practice Aid, Assets Acquired in a Purchase Business Combination to Be Used in Research and Development Activities. (sic: Assets Acquired in a Business Combination to Be Used in Research and Development Activities: A Focus on Software, Electronic Devices, and Pharmaceutical Industries)
    b. Review the reconciliation of the valuation to the purchase price paid.
    c. [This information is normally found in the "valuation analysis" section of the valuation report.]
    d. Consider whether other intangibles exist to which a portion of the purchase has not been allocated.
    [The report should identify and value all intangibles acquired (when several specialists are used to value intangibles, there may be more than one report, but identifiable intangibles should be valued).]
6. If the income approach to valuation is used, review the cash flow forecasts and consider whether the significant assumptions applied to the projects in process are unreasonable. Among the more significant assumptions are the following:
    a. Potential for introduction of new technologies that may obsolete the acquired technology

Exhibit 7.3   *(Continued)*

---

    b. Likelihood of project completion

    c. Estimates of stage of completion and time to completion

    d. Cost to complete

    e. Product life cycle and technology development strategies

    f. Expected sales volumes, product pricing, and expected revenues (exclusive of amounts attributable to contributory assets and core technology)

    g. Production and other costs (exclusive of the effects of buyer synergies)

    h. Discount rates

    i. Competitors' expected prices

7. Test the data furnished to the valuation specialist as follows:

    a. Assess the relative importance of IPR&D to the acquisition by considering the materials reviewed during the planning procedures as well as other materials, such as presentations to the Board, white papers, and due diligence working papers.

    b. Test the mathematical accuracy of the forecasts furnished to the specialist.

    c. Determine whether cash flow estimated were developed using "market participant" assumptions. With respect to "market participant" assumptions, paragraph 1.1.16 of the AICPA Practice Aid states:

       . . . For purposes of assigning cost to the assets acquired in accordance with APB Opinion 16, the amount of the purchase price allocated to an acquired identifiable intangible asset would not include any entity-specific synergistic value. Fair value does not include strategic or synergistic value resulting from expectations about future events that are specific to a particular buyer because the value associated with those components are unique to the buyer and seller and would not constitute market-based assumptions. As such, entity-specific value associated with strategic or synergistic components would be included in goodwill. Fair value would incorporate expectations about future events that affect market participants. If the acquiring company concludes that the discounted cash flow method best approximates the fair value of an acquired identifiable intangible asset, the discounted cash flows would incorporate assumptions that market participants would use in their estimates of future revenues and future expenses. (sic)

       [A footnote to paragraph 1.1.16 refers readers to current developments in accounting related to market participant assumptions.]

    d. Consider the amounts of R&D costs expended to date and estimated remaining completion costs for reasonableness.

    e. Review descriptions of the milestones achieved and compare the status with the actual costs incurred and projected remaining costs.

    f. Consider whether IPR&D is related to products that will be marketed externally.

    g. Inquire of appropriate client personnel whether IPR&D has achieved technological feasibility (or the equivalent) and has no alternative future use.

8. Evaluate the overall results of the valuation. Consider:

    a. Whether the size of the IPR&D charge is consistent with the overall nature of the business and management's purchase rationale.

    b. The size of the existing base (or core) technology value relative to the IPR&D value is reasonable.

Exhibit 7.3 *(Continued)*

c. The reasonableness of the IPR&D value with respect to the extent of completion efforts remaining.

d. Whether the IPR&D value will be realizable and whether both the buyer and seller are compensated considering the risks.

e. Major milestones achieved in the IPR&D project as of the purchase date and their consistency with the valuation.

f. The entire purchase price allocation reflects the acquiring company's technology, industry position, age, reputation, and strategic plan.

9. Obtain a representation letter from the client that includes the following:

   a. Management agrees with the findings of the valuation specialist.

   b. The IPR&D assets have substance, are incomplete, and have no alternative future use.

   c. The historical financial data provided to the valuation specialist was prepared on a basis consistent with the audited financial statements.

   d. Forecasts and other estimates provided to the valuation specialist are consistent with those developed for other parties or for internal use. The forecasts of future cash flows used in the valuation represent management's best estimate of future conditions consistent with the assumptions specified in the specialist's valuation using market participant assumptions rather that those that are entity specific (see the footnote to paragraph 1.1.16 of the AICPA Practice Aid).

   e. Under the traditional approach, the discount rate applied to estimated future net cash flows appropriately reflects the nature and complexity of the remaining development effort and the amount and timing of estimated expenditures necessary to complete the development of the IPR&D projects.

10. Determine that information requiring separate disclosure in the financial statements is properly identified in the working papers and presented in the financial statements, including the disclosures identified in paragraph 4.2 of the AICPA Practice Aid.

Conclusion

Based on the procedures performed, we are satisfied that our working papers appropriately document that acquired IPR&D does not contain any material misstatements, in relation to the financial statements taken as a whole. Exceptions are attached or stated below.

_____

_____

Endnotes

Chapter 1 History of Mergers and Acquisitions and Financial Reporting

1. Accounting Principles Board, APB Opinion No. 17, *Intangible Assets* (August 1970) at 27.
2. Ibid, at 9.
3. Applied Financial Information, LP, *Mergerstat® Review 2001* (Los Angeles, CA: 2001), p. 9.
4. Accounting Principles Board, APB Opinion No. 16, *Business Combinations* (August 1970), at 11.
5. Ibid., at 12.
6. Ibid., at 11.
7. Ibid., at 12.
8. Accounting Principles Board, APB Opinion No. 17, *Intangible Assets* (August 1970), at 27–31.
9. Accounting Principles Board, APB Opinion No. 16, *Business Combinations* (August 1970), at 46–48.
10. Ibid., at 16.
11. Ibid., at 18–21.
12. Accounting Principles Board, APB Opinion No. 17, *Intangible Assets* (August 1970), at 1–9.
13. Ibid., at 27.
14. Financial Accounting Standards Board, Statement of Financial Accounting Standards No. 141, *Business Combinations* (June 2001), Appendix B.
15. *Newark Morning Ledger Co. v. U.S.*, 734 F Supp. 176 (D.N.J. 1990) cited in Consulting Services Practice Aid 99-2, *Valuing Intellectual Property and Calculating Infringement Damages*, AICPA p. 99.
16. House of Representatives, H.R. 5365 IH, "Financial Accounting for Intangibles Reexamination (FAIR) Act," 106th Congress, 2d Session, (October 3, 2000).
17. Hopkins, et al., "Purchase, Pooling, and Equity Analysts' Valuation Judgments," *The Accounting Review*, Vol. 75, No. 3 (July 2000), pp. 260–261.
18. Ibid., pp. 261–262.
19. Ibid., pp. 276–277.
20. Ibid., p. 270.

21. Stephen Taub, *AOL: You've Got Impairment*, CFO.com, (January 8, 2002).
22. Roy Harris and Jennifer Caplan, *The Perils of Impairment*, CFO.com, (January 1, 2002).
23. Chris Ayres, "US Set for $1 Trillion of Internet Writeoffs," *The Times*, (January 10, 2002), http://www.thetimes.co.uk.
24. Ibid.
25. Craig Schneider, *Pool's Closed*, CFO.com, (June 29, 2001).
26. PriceWaterhouseCoopers, *Shedding Light on the New Business Combination Rules—A Guide for Deal Makers*, Executive Summary.
27. Bear Stearns, *Goodbye, Goodwill* (June 2001), p. 9.
28. Ibid.
29. Ibid.
30. Ibid.
31. Financial Accounting Standards Board, Exposure Draft, *Business Combinations and Intangible Assets* (September 1999), at 52.
32. Hopkins et al., "Purchase, Pooling, and Equity Analysts' Valuation Judgments," *The Accounting Review*, Vol. 75, No. 3 (July 2000) p. 276.

Chapter 2   Goodwill and Other Intangible Assets in a Business Combination

1. Margaret Blair and Steven Wallman, *Unseen Wealth: Report of the Brookings Task Force on Intangibles* (Washington, DC: Brookings Institution Press, 2001), p. 3.
2. International Valuation Standards, Guidance Note No. 4, *Intangible Assets* (2001), at 3.15.
3. Financial Accounting Standards Board, Statement of Financial Standards No. 141: *Business Combinations* (June 2001), p. 124.
4. Margaret Blair and Steven Wallman, *Unseen Wealth: Report of the Brookings Task Force on Intangibles* (Washington, DC: Brookings Institution Press, 2001), p. 15.
5. Michael Mard, *Task Force Report to Business Valuation Subcommittee* (2000).
6. FASB Proposal for a New Agenda Project, *Disclosure of Information about Intangible Assets Not Recognized in Financial Statements* (2001).
7. Ibid.
8. Baruch Lev, *Intangibles: Management, Measurement and Reporting* (Washington, DC: Brookings Institution Press, 2001), p. 22.
9. Ibid., p. 23.
10. Financial Accounting Standards Board, Statement of Financial Accounting Standards, No. 141: *Business Combinations* (June 2001), at 14.
11. Ibid., at A14.
12. Ibid., at 39.

13. Michael Mard and Joseph Agiato, Jr., Consulting Services Practice Aid 99-2: *Valuing Intellectual Property and Calculating Infringement Damages* (New York: AICPA, 1999), at 1.15.
14. International Valuation Guidance Note No. 6, *Business Valuation* (July 2000), at 6.3.
15. Ibid., at 6.7.
16. Baruch Lev, *Intangibles: Management, Measurement and Reporting* (Washington, DC: Brookings Institution Press, 2001), p. 39.
17. Financial Accounting Standards Board, Statement of Financial Accounting Standards No. 141: *Business Combinations* (June 2001), Appendix F.
18. Internal Revenue Service, Revenue Ruling 59-60, § 2.02.
19. Financial Accounting Standards Board, Statement of Financial Accounting Standards No. 141: *Business Combinations* (June 2001), at 9.
20. Ibid., at 13–15.
21. Ibid., at 43.
22. Ibid., Appendix F.
23. Ibid., at 39.
24. Financial Accounting Standards Board, Statement of Financial Accounting Standards No. 142, *Goodwill and Other Intangible Assets* (June 2001), at 11–14.
25. Financial Accounting Standards Board, Statement of Financial Concepts No. 7, *Using Cash Flow Information and Present Value in Accounting Measurements* (February 2000), at 40.
26. Ibid., at 39.
27. Randy J. Larson, et al., *Assets Acquired in a Business Combination to Be Used in Research and Development Activities: A Focus on Software, Electronic Devices, and Pharmaceutical Industries* (New York: AICPA, 2001), at 5.3.83.
28. Ibid., Introduction, p. x.
29. Ibid., at 3.2.04.
30. Ibid., at 3.2.02.
31. Financial Accounting Standards Board, Statement of Financial Accounting Concepts No. 6, *Elements of Financial Statements*, (December 1985), pp. 25–26.
32. Randy J. Larson, et al., *Assets Acquired in a Business Combination to Be Used in Research and Development Activities: A Focus on Software, Electronic Devices, and Pharmaceutical Industries* (New York: AICPA, 2001), at 3.3.14.
33. Ibid., at 3.3.26.
34. Ibid., at 3.3.40.
35. Ibid., at 3.3.42.
36. Ibid., at 3.3.55.
37. Ibid., at 4.2.

38. Ibid., at 1.1.08.
39. Ibid., at 1.1.16.
40. Ibid., at 5.3.29.
41. Ibid., at 5.2.08.
42. Ibid., at 5.3.11.
43. Ibid., at 5.3.33.
44. Ibid.
45. Ibid.

Chapter 3   Determining Goodwill and Other Intangible Assets in a Business Combination: A Case Study

1. Financial Accounting Standards Board, Statement of Financial Accounting Standards No. 141, *Business Combinations* (June 2001), at 13.
2. Financial Accounting Standards Board, Statement of Financial Accounting Standards No. 141, *Business Combinations* (June 2001), at 20.
3. American Society of Appraisers, *Business Valuation Standards* (2001), p. 24.
4. SFAS No. 141 prohibits assembled workforce from recognition as an intangible asset apart from goodwill. However, the asset is valued here to provide a basis for a return in the excess earnings methodology. Its value is included in goodwill in the final analysis.
5. Financial Accounting Standards Board, Statement of Financial Accounting Standards No. 142, *Goodwill and Other Intangible Assets* (June 2001), at 11.
6. Ibid.
7. Randy J. Larson, et al., *Assets Acquired in a Business Combination to Be Used in Research and Development Activities: A Focus on Software, Electronic Devices, and Pharmaceutical Industries* (New York: AICPA, 2001), at 5.2.07.
8. I.R.C. § 197(a) (July 1991).
9. Shannon P. Pratt, *Cost of Capital, Estimation and Applications* (New York: John Wiley & Sons, Inc., 1998), p. 46.
10. For example, see *Cost of Capital, Estimation and Applications*, by Shannon P. Pratt, CFA, FASA, CBA (New York: John Wiley & Sons, Inc. 1998), and *Financial Valuation*, by James R. Hitchner, CPA/ABV, ASA (New York: John Wiley & Sons, Inc., to be published Fall 2002).
11. Robert F. Reilly and Robert P. Schweihs, *Valuing Intangible Assets* (New York: McGraw-Hill, 1999), p. 122.
12. Ibid.
13. Financial Accounting Standards Board, Statement of Financial Accounting Standards No. 141, *Business Combinations* (June 2001), at 39.

14. Randy J. Larson, et al., *Assets Acquired in a Business Combination to Be Used in Research and Development Activities: A Focus on Software, Electronic Devices, and Pharmaceutical Industries* (New York: AICPA, 2001), at 5.3.64.

15. Ibid.

16. For example, *Valuing Intangible Assets*, by Robert F. Reilly and Robert P. Schweihs (New York: McGraw-Hill, 1999).

17. Randy J. Larson, et al., *Assets Acquired in a Business Combination to Be Used in Research and Development Activities: A Focus on Software, Electronic Devices, and Pharmaceutical Industries* (New York: AICPA, 2001), at 5.3.47.

18. In this model, the cost to complete is forecast as an additional expense that bears the risk of the asset overall. Some practitioners believe the cost to complete is a known expenditure that should be discounted at a lower rate, perhaps even a risk-free rate.

19. Financial Accounting Standards Board, Statement of Financial Accounting Standards No. 141, *Business Combinations* (June 2001), at B169.

Chapter 4   SFAS No. 142, Impairment of Goodwill and Other Intangible Assets

1. Financial Accounting Standards Board, Statement of Financial Accounting Standards, No. 142, *Goodwill and Other Intangible Assets* (June 2001), at 17–18.

2. Ibid., at 31.

3. Ibid., at 23, footnote 16.

4. Ibid., at 32.

5. Ibid., at 34.

6. Ibid., at 39.

7. Ibid., at 27.

8. Ibid., at 28.

9. Ibid., Appendix F.

10. Financial Accounting Standards Board, Statement of Financial Accounting Standards No. 141, *Business Combinations* (June 2001), at B102.

11. Ibid., at B103–B105.

12. Financial Accounting Standards Board, Statement of Financial Accounting Standards No. 142, *Goodwill and Other Intangible Assets* (June 2001), at 12.

13. Ibid., at 11.

14. Ibid., at 17.

15. Ibid., at 23–25.

16. Ibid., at 24.
17. Ibid., at 20–21.
18. Ibid., at 29.
19. Ibid., at 54–58.
20. Ibid., at 44.
21. Ibid., at 44.
22. Ibid., at 45.
23. Ibid.
24. Ibid., at 47.
25. Ibid.
26. Ibid.

Chapter 5 Impairment Analysis: A Case Study

1. Financial Accounting Standards Board, Statement of Financial Accounting Standards No. 142, *Goodwill and Other Intangible Assets* (June 2001), at 19.
2. Ibid., at 20.
3. Ibid., at 19.
4. Ibid., at 23.
5. Financial Accounting Standards Board, Statement of Financial Accounting Standards No. 144, *Accounting for the Impairment or Disposal of Long-Lived Assets* (August 2001), at 7.
6. Ibid., at 8.
7. Financial Accounting Standards Board, Statement of Financial Accounting Standards No. 142, *Goodwill and Other Intangible Assets* (June 2001), at 29.
8. Financial Accounting Standards Board, Statement of Financial Accounting Standards No. 144, *Accounting for the Impairment or Disposal of Long-Lived Assets* (August 2001), at 22.
9. Financial Accounting Standards Board, Statement of Financial Accounting Standards No. 142, *Goodwill and Other Intangible Assets* (June 2001), at 29.
10. Some practitioners believe that, under the fair value standard, the Section 197 amortization of intangible assets should be recalculated assuming an acquisition of the company occurred as of the date of the impairment test, resulting in a new amortization calculation and a new 15-year tax life.
11. Financial Accounting Standards Board, Statement of Financial Accounting Standards No. 142, *Goodwill and Other Intangible Assets* (June 2001), at 23.

Chapter 6   Issues in and Implementation of SFAS Nos. 141 and 142

1. Financial Accounting Standards Board, Discussion of Agenda Projects as of January 1, 2002, *Business Combinations*, http://www.fasb.org/tech/buscomb.html.

2. Ibid.

3. Financial Accounting Standards Board, *Business Combinations: Purchase Method Procedures*, March 27, 2002, http://www.fasb.org/project/bc_purchasemethod.html.

4. Ibid.

5. Financial Accounting Standards Board, FASB Staff Announcement, Topic No. D-100.

6. Financial Accounting Standards Board, Statement of Financial Accounting Standards No. 141, *Business Combinations* (June 2001), at 44–45.

7. Financial Accounting Standards Board, Statement of Financial Accounting Standards No. 142, *Goodwill and Other Intangible Assets* (June 2001), at 40.

8. Accounting Principles Board, APB Opinion No. 18, *The Equity Method of Accounting for Investments in Common Stock* (March 1971), at 19(h).

9. Financial Accounting Standards Board, *Business Combinations: New Business Accounting*, February 7, 2002, http://www.fasb.org/project/bc_newbasis.html.

10. Financial Accounting Standards Board, *Combinations of Not-for-Profit Organizations*, January 23, 2002, http://www.fasb.org/project/nfp.html.

11. Ibid.

Index